THE SHOPFLOOR MAN

For a complete list of Management Books 2000 titles,
visit our web-site at http://www.mb2000.com

THE SHOPFLOOR MAN

Peter Sinclair

2000

All royalties from sales of this book are being donated to Enable (MENCAP).

Published in 1999 by Management Books 2000 Ltd
Cowcombe House,
Cowcombe Hill,
Chalford,
Gloucestershire GL6 8HP
Tel. 01285-760722 Fax: 01285-760708
e-mail: MB2000@compuserve.com

Printed and bound in Great Britain by Biddles, Guildford

British Library Cataloguing in Publication Data is available

ISBN 1-85252-298-4

CONTENTS

1

INTRODUCTION

In the beginning, God created Heaven and Earth...

So, you may read no further!

Most books on management elaborate a few basic ideas to excess, merely to satisfy the need for a new book. If only they would distil what they have to say into a few coherent bullet-points, perhaps with one or two vivid illustrations and a plan diagram, then the superfluous narrative need not distract us from the core message. The ideas could be absorbed and used as a basis for implementation in your own way, in your own situation, allowing you to build-in some sort of individuality and originality pertinent to your circumstances; and the inevitable result would be... *Instant success!*

Other books, those by entrepreneurs in particular, tell of the wheeling and dealing, the glamour and the glory (usually that which attaches only to the author) and treat the mundane process of actually manufacturing a product as an inanimate object in itself. In many cases, manufacturing is not even the be-all and end-all of the business: a perfect balance sheet is usually the desired Nirvana, and to hell with the process.

Yet other management books rely on stereotypical characters, heavily disguised (presumably) to protect the innocent; and on annoyingly pat 'case histories' that are usually anything but, reflecting as they do only credit on the author and (usually) his brilliant organisational qualities.

Virtually all business books, however, are about 'SUCCESS!!!' How to achieve it, how to recognise it, how to live with it... At this point, perhaps, I should apologise, for this book is largely about real life, about developing and growing; and how, by working with people and all their foibles, we eventually progress. Success is not to be had overnight: there are no 'magic bullets', whatever the Consultants may say (fewer than 30 per cent of 're-engineering' projects succeed in meeting their business objectives!)

In that sense, it is more recognisably true to our human evolution and history; the product of experience, rather than a fictional work of the imagination.

People needing people

If the truth be told, most books on business are written by and for the ego: bought mostly by the author himself for distribution among his intimate friends and business acquaintances – if he is desperate enough, his customers, even... or used for promotional purposes at prestigious international gatherings, where to be without a new book is akin to arriving at a posh garden party in Bermuda shorts.

And yet, all management books seem to agree on one thing: *people* are important. People matter. People 'make the difference'. Mine/ours, they say, is a 'people business'... Nowadays, you have to 'bring your people with you'; give them 'ownership' of any idea, however embarrassing; 'empower' them (ghastly expression, of which more later...), pander to their 'inner child' and motivate their innate creativity... Before, presumably, you fire them and achieve the perfect balance sheet. (I know, the politically correct buzz word is 'outplace'. Balls!).

So, what about the *people* in my book? Turners, vertical millers, horizontal borers, C.N.C. operators, toolmakers...These are the real people who, we are told, 'matter' in the factitious world of business books.

I am not talking here about 'businesses' like advertising or 'P.R.', banking and financial services, fast food, the 'heritage' industry (mostly earlier failures which didn't lurch on to success), or call centres, all of which are rapidly replacing the real process of wealth creation in this country. I am talking about the living remnants of our once-great industry. These real people have real concerns and worries no less important to them than the managing director or chairman.They have a real contribution to make to the management of a business, often knowing more about it from an operational point of view, if only in making it bloody nearly impossible: for, in the real world of manufacturing and engineering, it is the shopfloor man who still keeps the wheels oiled and turning, or not, as the case may be; not all the accountants, consultants, P.R. men, M.B.A.'s and head hunters in Christendom.

Heroes and villains

That is why the heroes and villains of my book are the shopfloor men. (And I'm sorry, ladies, but they are, to a man, with all their faults plainly men; hence the use of the masculine pronoun throughout...) Not only that, but I have used (by kind permission, of course, and with only one thinly-disguised exception) real people, with real names and real lives, real talents and real personality disorders – and sometimes almost unbearably real personal relationships, both to me and others – to illuminate my treatise.

For, while God created Heaven and Earth, it was my dad who created... *Main Tool*!

Just the business

My father wanted me to become an accountant.He started Main Tool in the early 1960s, after quitting the mining industry through ill-health, and conned his way into an engineering firm. Not that he was a con man: he was as honest as the day is long.But needs must, and after becoming tool room manager, he started up his own small business in the machine room, behind the chippy in Main Street, Bellshill. Hence the name, Main Tool.

He did well, those were boom times for mechanical engineering, and it was a cash-rich business.But he wanted something better for me, and I was sent off to accountancy school. I lasted a year, before the double-entry bookkeeping drove me round the bend, and I went back into the bosom of the family business. I did my apprenticeship, somewhat late in life, got a qualification, worked hard, married, had a family, and – just to prove I wasn't stupid – finally did my degree in engineering and management. I went to work for Rolls Royce for a while, but then my father died and left the business to my uncles.They were doing as well as can be expected, but there comes a time when the extended family concept ceases to hold up as a paradigm of sound business practice. In a nutshell, the business lost direction, and it came to me that it was my unfortunate lot in life to step in and do something.

I suppose you would not call us a conventional family. My younger brother Alan runs the Wise Group, a fantastic organisation which creates job opportunities for long-term unemployed people.My sister Irene is also a trustee of the business, but the secret as far as I was concerned was that one man should be in charge, and that man was me! Consequently, our constitution was designed to leave me to run the business in my own way unless I was to make an almighty mess of it, which so far...

After gently moving the uncles aside, effectively banishing all forms of nepotism, I invested some money in new technology, computer-controlled C.N.C. cutting equipment, as you will find described in the narrative which follows. We also invested a lot of time, trouble and patience in business initiatives and consultants. We were up to our necks in consultants; but somehow, we still didn't seem to see that guiding light which all enterprises need to find, once the initial spark of creation has fizzled out. All I knew was, the solution had to lie within the business, and the oddball collection of highly-skilled machinists we employed, and still (mostly) do. This book, then, is dedicated to these heroes and (occasional) villains.

2

THE SHOPFLOOR MAN

Funnily enough, you don't often read a management book that is about shopfloor workers. Is this because the world of the shopfloor man is still in Britain, unlike in Japan, utterly divorced, culturally, financially, linguistically, from that of the officers' mess? If so, and I believe this book shows that there is still a yawning gulf fixed, although I believe that it can and (obviously) must be bridged, then what on earth use is it, writing yet another academic, 'management' textbook, as if managers were a separate species of human being, as many seem to think they are?

Surely, at some point, a connection has to be made between theory and practice? Between the theoretical, analytical, figures-driven, 'performance-related' world of the upstairs office, and the real world of oily, noisy, recalcitrant machines and their (sometimes) equally difficult and impenetrable minders, whose one overriding concern is not so much financial performance indicators as keeping up the overtime?

And is sending out one hundred letters of redundancy one hundred times more difficult than having one man sitting in front of you at a table, crying because you are making him redundant? I think not. For a hundred men, a working community, the emotional conflict for them is far greater than that of the high-powered manager behind the table, whose 'buck' stops with the shareholders. For him, there's safety – and anonymity – in numbers. So, let's get down to the nitty gritty of dealing with real, individual human beings.

Native intelligence

This book is about Change Management, right enough – but I prefer to think of it as how the Hell do you make it work, using real people? That's the really big challenge of management in our 'Change Culture'... I'll deal later with the problems of interacting with a group of people in a shopfloor environment, and of coping with their quick, native (perhaps also naive?) intelligence, as well as their skills, quirks, hang-ups – and hangovers.

This book is also about my own, mostly frustrated attempts at management development: at turning raw machinists into 'managers with vision', for my business purpose. After all, do not the best management textbooks say this is the future? Handy's 'cloverleaf company': flat, green, widely-distributed and lucky for some...

Bubble theory – an introduction

Herein and throughout, I have used my own, idiosyncratic definition of management which I thought best suited to what I was trying to do in the business:

MANAGEMENT = RUNNING THE SYSTEM +.

The 'plus' I've added at the end covers all those non-operational, non-analytical, not-involved-with-counting-things (but nonetheless critical) aspects of management which are relevant to the individual being managed, and to do with developing his or her present and future role within the company.

This none-too profound perception, which has gratifyingly been written about elsewhere and in the press, culminated in what has come to be known as Sinclair's Bubble theory. (Sadly, it has not also brought me Tom Peters' annual income, but my P.R. team are working on it.) I have now granted 'ownership' of my theory to all and sundry, as it seemed the best way of encouraging the work force to take it on board. So we can drop the 'Sinclair' bit, it's just Bubble theory and it's in the public domain. So much so, that industrialists flock from miles around to find out about it for themselves.

Forever growing bubbles

Put simply, because it is simple, unbelievably so, every worker operates within a 'bubble' of personal and operational concerns that make up his daily round. As their bubble grows, the individual rises, eventually maybe right to the top and out and beyond...

It is the job of management to support the growth of people's individual bubbles, to be in a sense even subservient to them. Bubbles of course begin with the individual, but can eventually break through to encompass larger areas of work, even whole business divisions, and contribute to the profitability of the business. The bigger and higher the bubble, the greater the level of responsibility is assumed by the individual; including responsibility for growing other people's bubbles, which is most important.

Of course, this sort of abstract theory could easily be conflated into one of those Buddhist management textbooks I talked about at the beginning. It has its mystical attractions. But actually, I wanted to write about my real experience of introducing; or, at least, trying to introduce, change, involving real people and machines in the real world of machine shop manufacturing. So we'll keep the Bubble theory firmly locked away in its special case for today, and start instead with the Dramatis Personae.

Here, then, are some of the people I have encountered running a subcontract machine shop, a business which my father started in his work room behind the fish and chip emporium in Main Street, Bellshill, Lanarkshire; people whom you will meet later during the course of my narrative. The only thing I have missed out is the bad language, because of course, unlike most Scottish industrialists,I don't swear.

3

DRAMATIS PERSONAE

Baillie Fraser – Jig Borer

All arguments with Baillie revert to:'It's all about going back to basics'. His basics are that all you have to do is bring the work in and he will make money from it. Nothing could be simpler.

Baillie is a proud man, politically somewhere to the right of Genghis Khan: an egocentric, a mason, a Unionist and a mercenary, he is a man of larger appetites. When he goes fishing, he catches more fish. When he goes drinking, he gets more drunk... His apprenticeship and training were conducted under a bonus system in which his aggressiveness in chasing 'thous' earned him top wages. Apart from his relatively high rate of pay, then, the only way for him to make *more* money was by working overtime.

As a company, we believed in profit sharing (we don't believe any more) – since the variations in the diverse range of work for the skilled man cannot be measured against a precedent. This unfortunately sets a ceiling on the individual aspirations of a man like Baillie Fraser, hence his pugnacious pursuit of better staff conditions. He will argue and fight for every penny. Away on a company seminar, for instance, he demanded vociferously that the men should receive time and a half for eating fillet steak and drinking malt whisky at the company's expense, out of normal working hours... I agreed to pay him overtime on condition he left the table. Needless to say, he stayed.

This inflexibility and pride of Baillie's are manifested in another minor hang-up: a total and obdurate resistance to change. The craft skills he has proudly acquired (and passed on with uncharacteristic generosity) over the past 25 years and more have been threatened by new technology, such as computer controlled machines. Although younger people have adapted to these necessary skills, Baillie's belief in a 'Back To Basics' philosophy to rival that of the former British Prime Minister, John Major, is defended on any and every occasion with a speech denigrating the new technology. This constant glorification of the old ways and instinctive, ostrich-like clinging to 'the basics' has inevitably resulted in Baillie being marked out as the company dinosaur. His power to influence outcomes has been severely curtailed, in fact, only since his area in the shop floor has become known to all and sundry as 'Jurassic Park'.

Fear of change

Now, fear of change is a straightforward man-management problem and, in most case studies, a successful solution would be found with consummate ease. For Baillie's development, the problem lies in simply overcoming the 'macho' mind-set which proclaims every change successfully resisted as a personal victory in a hostile world. With his undoubtedly high level of skill, ability and industriousness, which are absolutely recognised by his colleagues, efforts were duly made to try and turn Baillie Fraser into a manager.

The first step was to put him in charge of apprentices. The reasoning behind this was as follows:

> Our company had a deplorable record of training apprentices, mainly because we had a laissez-faire approach to most things. This benefited neither the apprentice nor the company. We agreed with the traditional way of training with, and learning

from, a skilled man. This approach has lost favour in larger organisations where a starter may be appointed to someone below average and therefore be taught inefficiency and bad practice. With our philosophy of maintaining the highest skills we had to cultivate them in house. Baillie's skills were the highest, and it was imperative that they be passed on.

We also felt it was right to try to make Baillie more managerial and to prise open his cocoon, enabling him to extend his skills at organising and controlling things. To his credit, he set up an excellent training programme and tempered his inclination to deride rather than praise his apprentices. On the whole, the programme is successful. How is it then that I still feel the experiment has been a failure? It is because nothing else has changed. Any discussions and meetings with Baillie still end up dispiritingly with his appealing to us to 'Get back to basics'. He has apparently made no effort, or, more probably, is simply never going to be capable, of expanding his outer vision to see the broader picture of a company with its own direction and strategy. He remains resolutely locked in the past,a prisoner of his own fear of the future.

Raymond Davies – Toolmaker

Raymond joined the company ten years ago. It was soon vividly apparent that he was extremely talented. What makes a skilled operator stand out from other skilled workers, and how to teach that ingredient to others, deserves full and proper analysis. A more tangible example of what I am talking about is when, on one occasion, Raymond succeeded in machining a sophisticated component in 90 minutes – a job which had previously taken another operative nine hours! The job apparently called for much time-consuming fixturing, based on numerous complex datum points, and the previous operative had proceeded logically, step-by-step, on the basis of sound technical knowledge. Wielding the famous Occam's Razor, Raymond, however, had simply taken one look at this complicated part, seized on the key datum point for the whole job and, bolting through it, had eliminated most of the complex technical input to crack the job in a tenth of the time. Clearly, there is a certain mind set which can create enormous value in an organisation by seeing with absolute clarity, right to the heart of even the most complex issues.

The problem which I have observed in top skilled people is not the clichéd 'prima donna' syndrome, but that in most cases a strong character is evident with attendant quirks... Raymond, for instance, would clock out of the factory if he did not have enough work. He would also threaten to leave (a common reaction with top men) if he did not get his overtime. He was not alone in maintaining this lofty attitude: I remember arguing with an uncle of the same ilk (nepotism ran rife in our family business), who finished his work on a surface grinder at 11 o'clock in the morning and blatantly read a book until the end of his shift. His argument was that he did more in three hours than anyone else did in eight, and he was not going to hide the fact. He was paid the same as them, he guaranteed he would always do more than anyone else, and that was his justification for doing nothing at all the rest of the time!

Making more space

Apart from the philosophical argument, the problem this sort of moral absolutism throws at you is how to motivate the talented but bored individual, within the constraints of the negative effect it would undoubtedly have on his colleagues if he were paid more than they.

It is generally the less able who are, in their own mind, worth more than they actually are. In a small shopfloor environment, where the structure of 'foreman and managers' are rigidly set by tradition, there is no obvious path of promotion for good men. Their 'Bubbles' are seldom allowed to grow, and eventually, they leave.

Strangely, I was never worried by Raymond's threat of leaving. It surprised me recently, when Raymond told me how I used to ask him challenging questions about things that had nothing to do with his job.

I can't recall asking any of these questions now, but I do know that I wanted to find out what he was made of. Knowing that he had the ability to be successful at anything he tackled, that binding knowledge was enough to give me confidence that I could convince him not to leave for another company. If he had wanted to go out on his own, which he was probably capable of, although uncertain about the risk to himself and his family, I would have backed him. This, I did not tell him.

We initially made Raymond a charge hand to look after the apprentices but it was not a real solution. I was only buying time. In truth, I could not find a way of fulfilling his potential. The frustration I felt also went for several other intelligent and capable people on the shop floor, for whom I could not find sufficient scope and opportunity within the business to 'grow their bubble'. How to resolve this particular problem became a crusade in my mind. I always remember the great middle distance runner, Brendan Foster, being interviewed and asked how it felt to be the best runner in Britain? He immediately replied with characteristic modesty that he did not necessarily think he was the best runner in Britain; other, better runners may not have had the same opportunities. How then was I to give my 'shopfloor men' the opportunity to run?

Jim Good – Machinist

Jim Good is better than good – he's wonderful, an employer's dream. Exemplary family man; a credit to society; a first-rate machinist with an entire tool kit of adaptable skills; a pleasant disposition; no 'side', and nothing is too much trouble.

He has that untapped intelligence, too. Leaving school at 15, having to go to work to help support a large but poor family, he took his apprenticeship in a small machine shop that happened to be close to his home in a small village, and after he decided to move on, we picked him up by recommendation. A recommendation that told us to take him on in spite of himself, of how he would appear at first meeting. This was canny advice because, when he arrived for his interview, he came across as totally lacking in self-confidence: bashful, apologetic and worried that he would not fulfil our expectations of him. Allied to his natural humility, it must have been his previous working environment that had not allowed him to develop a clearer picture of his own worth. For, he turned out to be more-than capable of a very wide range of tasks. Milling, jig boring, grinding and any other discipline which might be required in a small machine shop, each was to us a valuable skill in its own right, but grist to his mill. Jim probably thought every tradesman was the same, for he had had no one to tell him otherwise. He was the proverbial 'flower born to blush unseen'.

We introduced Jim to C.N.C. (computer controlled) milling, as he was so keen to learn. It wasn't long before he became our best C.N.C. machining centre operator. He was also rated highly by his peers, both in ability and character, which is not always easy on the shop floor – it can be a hard apprenticeship, and a lot of honest men have foundered.

Jim was almost too good to be true. He did not put pressure on the management when work was slow and overtime cut, as he readily understood that we do not live and work in Utopia Plc. He would obligingly take his floating holidays when things were slack, and was genuinely horrified when work became scarce and the other top men on the floor wanted us to pay the weaker ones off so they could still get their overtime.

For the others, the 'Just go out and get more work' syndrome was hard to deal with. They did not want to know about those unpredictable external forces affecting the industry, little things like economic recession or your customers going out of business. They wanted to lash out at the company bosses for not letting them have their 'two nights and a Sunday' – it was always 'incompetent management' who were to blame for any downturn. There was no apparent sympathy whatever with the real dynamics of a business, how it interacts with other sectors of the economy, and how you have to control your costs according to the flow of work.

Now, I do not believe that those men really thought keeping a business running and orders flowing could be as easy as going down to Quicksave and picking groceries off the shelf – though sometimes, it seemed they did. It was just the macho way to go on. Jim, however, was completely understanding of the fact that we could not just go out and get more work if a market did not exist for our products. Instead, with the simplicity of intelligence and pure logic, he put forward his own solutions. Why didn't we target Aberdeen and the oil industry, where there was work? It would surely have been incompetent of management to ask on these occasions, 'Oh yeah, how?', because I am sure Jim would have told us! He had that clear logic and focus that ought to be inherent in good management.

Although he was a glaringly obvious candidate for promotion, and no one deserved it better, Jim's case presented me with certain problems. Some of the older-established charge hands saw him not only as a threat, with distinct prospects of getting on better than themselves – but also as a management pet; and management association, by tradition, was distrusted. The sub-culture would set out to shackle him, and it was up to me to find a way forward. But how?

David McLaughlin – Charge Hand

David wants to be a bastard. He actually specifies the type – a mean one. I have suggested it may be better to be a clever one. If he does not stop taking cream in his coffee and start running around Strathclyde park of a Saturday morning there is a distinct possibility he may become a fat one. Why does a nice boy like David want to become a bastard at all?

David as a mean one does not sit easily on the mind. He is obliging, friendly, amenable and the personification of a nice person. He is, however, pragmatic and wants to succeed. This, I fear, is the source of the bastardisation of David. He has been promoted to a position where he has to manage his work-mates and friends. Being intelligent, he knows and has seen, as everyone has for instance at the most glaring level of football, where a John Greig has to learn to manage his team mates, the need to distance himself from those he is paid to lead. The pitfalls and problems of promotion to management, so obvious to us all, are no less obvious to David. He needs to gain credibility. He has to win respect. He would probably like a sign made, telling the world he's in charge. In spite of this it still worries and perturbs me that he feels the need to become a bastard in order to make the transition.

Is his role model of the typical managerial bastard me, by any chance? Never ever, ever have I been one of those! Does he perhaps perceive it as the conventional culture in our entrepreneurial industry in these tough times, that you have got to be one to succeed? I think not. I think David wants to be a bastard because it focuses his mind on his ultimate objective. He wants, plain and simply, to succeed, and he is going to do it his way. Lord Elton put it another way: power corrupts.

This single-mindedness may be, and often is, a characteristic of success in business. It's not very attractive. I am perturbed that David may become cold, unfeeling and clinical. He does not suffer fools gladly; but have we not all at times fooled ourselves and needed guidance out of our foolishness? His men may be cynical and disparaging, but should he not temper their cynicism and win them over with his patient and humorous charm, instead of crystallising the worst characteristics of a 'J.R. Ewing' merely to prove that he is better then them? I would prefer David as a charmer rather than a cynic.

David as a clever bastard could still be a mean one if he had to be, without anyone realising. He can still be focused and mean but in the realisation of this meanness he can modify his leadership and approach to disguise this unyielding and precarious trait. Academic management teaching postulates that often, authoritarian leadership can easily flip into laissez-faire mode just to compensate. David does not need just to issue orders and do things without explanation, as it has already been established that his men are not brainless and can be led. Child psychologists are always telling us that you have to explain to a child why you are tanning its hide. David at least owes this to an intelligent adult. There are many ways of skinning a cat and it would be in everyone's interest if he did it the least painful way.

My biggest worry is that he will sit and wait and complain that nobody is doing anything. He may even become a lazy bastard in the end. I hope not.

Stewart Miller – Maintenance Man

Stewart Miller is big, strong, dark, taciturn and sour, and I am not the only one who is afraid of him. To my credit the rest are shit scared too. He can lift more with one hand than I can lift with both. When he was about to be married, Joe our storeman asked innocently where he was going to live after he was married. Stewart challenged him: 'What the f*** has it got to do wi' you?' Stewart practices and encourages this. The psychology, I think, is the feeling of power he can gain and maybe there is the chance that we would all enjoy it. If, however, you catch him with his guard down, he is as nice as ninepence. But if you rouse him he will rip your head off even if it means his job. He was not, however, included in the original batch of gremlins.

When he first applied for a job he was a marine engineer with a higher national diploma, who was prepared to take a labourer's rate to get a job and prove himself, as we did not have a need for a full time maintenance man. He is one of those people with whom I am always impressed as he seems to be able to do any job asked of him with confidence. When you ask him if he can do a job you almost see the brain going into clockwork; a delayed response then, '…aye'.

He will take the largest machine in the factory to bits and, no matter what is wrong, fix it. I am supposed to be an engineer but I could never do that. As well as being in charge of maintenance, I made him a quality engineer because we did need one of those. What I did not know and never thought to ask was what he himself actually wanted to do; but, as he did not communicate and remained the Prince of Darkness, as he was soon dubbed, it might have been difficult to find out. This reticence of his has hidden the fact that he is capable of so much more and is probably bored, perfecting his Christopher Lee persona for his own entertainment.

Peter Tait – Vertical Miller

Peter is a dissident, a classic Socialist. Articulate, embittered,he can fulfil the role of the morally righteous one with logic and heart. For most of his working life the trade union movement held his commitment at the expense of his own career and opportunity. Peter has the potential to be a manager in any company. He has now split from the union and is left still working a milling machine, even though we made him a charge hand. It is recognised in the company that he should most probably be doing a manager's job, but it is not in his way.

Peter represents the conventional Marxist view of 'company versus employee',in which permanent conflict of interest reins and never the twain shall meet. As an employer who has never exactly been a disciple of the 'team work' principal, I quite enjoy standing on this particular bridge of extremity. Apart from a perpetual obsession with improving working conditions, the universal Socialist argument is why should employers get the wealth and the workers only a wage? I could try and convince him with the usual owner-manager platitudes. I work harder; I have more responsibility; I worry more at night; I take more risks; It's my money and mortgage that underpin the business... Unfortunately, this is mostly rubbish. The most difficult job in our company is machining. For instance, a part costing £1,000 has to have this value added to it by obtaining accuracy within one thousandth of an inch. This requires skill, worry and pressure – and no future, once it's out the door. Workers invest just as much in any business as the bosses do, possibly more, as they have less to gain and everything to lose by failing. They are also dependant, by tradition, on those sleepless, worried, over-mortgaged and overpaid bosses for their livelihood – which is a source of worry in itself.

I can only say to Peter that he is probably absolutely right, but the system is like that, God made me the manager and I am lucky to be on this side. I just have to try and achieve the best for the company and its employees.

On-time delivery

Another management issue arose through Peter not being paid the top rate for a skilled man, although he was one. The reason was that he never started work on time. This was a fault with management but, with 20 years of precedence, nothing was done. We wanted him to start work on time and if he did we would pay him the top rate. Peter wanted the top rate first, then he would act accordingly and start on time. Probably against conventional management practice we agreed to pay him because we trusted him and he did not betray that trust. Would your company have done the same? It is a question of accommodation, and a rigid system would not make room for a Peter Tait, however skilled or talented.

Peter's trust is typical of people on the shop floor. The management give trust and it is rarely abused. We have an open store policy and I don't think you would be able to tell the difference between the efforts of supervised, as against unsupervised, shopfloor workers. Our supervision is just the oil to keep the process going.

These are the shopfloor men I have put my faith in and who have become my personal challenge, for: 'Many a flower is born to blush unseen and waste its sweetness on the desert air'.

4

CONSULTANTS

Over the years, we have had our share of consultants. A provocative statement from one of them confounded me. He was claiming that we could become a £50 million company and the only thing preventing it happening was me...

I later realised that they all use this classic opening gambit to pander to their clients' ego. It also helps their cause to wave a big number around, possibly so their fees seem small by comparison. At the time, however, it seemed rather a simplistic view of the business, as if there were some magic wand that could be waved and Securicor would start delivering money by the sackful, but it did at least jolt me into the realisation that it was up to me to do something about our future, and that was the start. There was not much inspiration going on inside the company, while outside there was a plethora of agencies and consultants all ready and waiting to do the inevitable S.W.O.T. diagram and tell us all the things we were doing wrong, for a fee. They were like flies around a camel's arse. I employed them for vision, they gave me strengths and weaknesses, opportunities and threats...

What all this analysis did do was to make it painfully obvious that our company, like so many in the engineering sector, was lacking in vision and enlightenment. Being preoccupied with survival in a declining manufacturing sector, we needed an environment which encouraged development and ideas. Being engineers, however, bound in logic, we lacked that freewheeling 'right-brain' creativity that sometimes produces quantum leaps to profitable change.

I duly attended a seminar on T.Q.M. (Total Quality Management). Being an awkward sod at heart, I told them that I could hardly go back and tell my work force what T.Q.M. was in a few short sentences when they, the consultants, couldn't manage to tell me after a whole day... One consultant thought he'd get his own back by telling me that the reason it had taken me a day to grasp the essentials was probably because I was thick. Under the pretence of needing someone better qualified to explain it for me, I promptly booked him to venture in to Main Tool and give us the benefit of his wisdom in person.

I wrote out a project brief for him, using as an example the problem that was still gnawing away at me, of how I could give more scope to a tradesman tied to a machine without causing even worse problems on the shopfloor. His conclusion, buried among all the T.Q.M. paraphernalia, was that we needed a cultural change. The seed was planted. The idea of a business having a 'culture' that can be 'changed' is old hat in management parlance now, although few have yet achieved it; but at the time, having that stark realisation confront me was challenging. I wanted and needed that challenge. I recognised the crying need for that change.

We waded through the ramifications of T.Q.M., with its 'personal development plans' and all the jargon about 'best practice', 'zero defects' and 'world class company'. We started on top management, who were to run with it under resistance until eventually, the initiative fizzled out. The charge hands and the shopfloor men were flatly not interested, much to the chagrin of Lawrie Spence, our consultant, who runs an outfit called Manufacturing Principles (I think it's supposed to be a pun, although you spell the other kind -als...). It was all 'rocket science', totally beyond their ken. It wasn't made of mild steel, that's for sure.

Lawrie, or 'H.G.V.' (Heavy Goods Vehicle) as he became known, came from a background and culture of large organisations such as

I.B.M., Compaq and I.C.I. As such, he was used to developing initiatives on a grand scale, working with managers in whom the processes and practices of management consultancy had been inculcated from birth. As befits an international athlete, he was extremely competitive and tough minded. It surprised me then that his method was to sweet talk you into discovering for yourself whatever it was he wanted you to discover. It took time for our charge hands to realise that this was going on, they were expecting to see immediate, tangible results. 'What work has he brought in?' 'What good is he doing the company?' These questions were constantly asked, of course in order to undermine the consultancy process – and because engineers in general simply do not like consultants in particular. Perhaps this is because engineers are designed to take responsibility for solving problems, while consultants merely highlight them, pocket their fees and vanish into the night.

I warned 'H.G.V.' ahead of time that the charge hands, intelligent men with strong views and unforgiving personalities, something which I encouraged rather than curbed, were not going to roll over and accept any fanciful flag waving initiative without question. Moreover, the commitment of having to produce to order has always been, by convention and circumstance, their primary motivation. The obvious worry that they would give any T.Q.M. initiative the cold shoulder, or insist, in their own words, that it was: 'A load of crap', did not bother me because, in my own mind, I was searching for something more. T.Q.M. was only the mist on the horizon of where we had to get to. We left the charge hands to their instinctive antagonism and returned to top management.

A 'people person'...

Being in the habit of wrapping myself up in technical matters and working at examination pace, I had completely neglected the man management side of the business. I now had to become a People Person – an odd notion, which people scoffed at because of what is sometimes said to be my abrasive nature. I realised that if I wanted people to change and develop, I would have to do the same. If I was persuading people to move out of their comfort zone, I had to move out of my comfort zone. At work, my comfort zone was doing the estimating. The more I had to do, the more I liked it because I did not have to think. It is extremely embarrassing when you give yourself time to think and then discover you have no brains to think with. On the personal side, I took up playing the fiddle even though I did not have a musical bone in my body. I worked diligently at it and eventually could manage 'Phil the Fluter's Ball'.

Still believing doggedly in the 'top-down' approach, we concentrated on the senior management development approach for some considerable time. It was painfully slow and, we eventually realised, getting us not much further down the road. When someone has being going on holiday to the same old caravan site for 36 years, as one of my colleagues had, it is unlikely – if not presumptuous to even think – that I could get him to try even a weekend mini-break on the Costa Brava.

The comfort zone argument continued for some time, especially on the shop floor. Someone doing a difficult, skilled and stressful job on a machine, a job which most people could not do, is inclined to react at the slightest suggestion of any hint of comfort there may be lurking in what was, after all, a man's job. We had to convince him that it was because he was so good at it, it was easier for him to do than for anyone else. It was more difficult and more uncomfortable to do a lesser job that he was not good at, than one he was. Thus, the comfort zone of a machinist might be physically hard, noisy and uncomfortable; but, 'pride in the job', and the sometimes cynical camaraderie of the shop floor, conspired to create a place where a man could feel sure of himself, and it was a hard place to break out of.

The argument from top management was not as strong: we all have our comfort zones, and a salary and a company car are pretty convincing ones. Maybe we took what appeared to be the easy option, although by convention and management teaching we were expected to do this anyway. What began to happen was a wee 'Hawthorn' experience.

Taking notice

The Hawthorn Experiment was a famous consultancy exercise, undertaken at the Western Electric Company's Hawthorn works in Chicago during the 1920s and 1930s. Initially, researchers were brought in to establish the optimum level of ambient lighting that would maximise productivity in all departments. However, they began to realise that something odd was going on. It seemed that, merely by asking questions, the researchers themselves were having a mysterious effect on productivity. It was not the lighting levels, as management had imagined, but the simple fact that someone was taking an interest in the views of the ordinary working folk, that stimulated the output of the work groups studied.

Elton Mayo, who was involved in the experiments, proposed that people have a deep need for recognition, security and belonging – and that these key motivators outshine even the lure of money. My challenge therefore was to develop people who were profoundly set in their ways, who had been reared in the solid, ethical tradition of 'managers manage and workers work', to encourage them to have and express their own ideas, to grow their own and others' spheres of responsibility, and to become managers with an entrepreneurial, individual spirit and a wider view of the company, its markets and prospects. Some vision! Instead, the charge hands merely became jealous and sulky. They wanted to receive the same attention as they saw the managers getting. So, it was back to the charge hands for 'H.G.V.', because all that expensive attention was getting us nowhere with management.

Lawrie, our consultant, talked to the group both individually and collectively under the theme of T.Q.M. (Total Quality Management) and continuous improvement. The murmurings from the men were not that encouraging. Some were open and willing to listen, but others were doubtful and even hostile. Those who were 'dead against' threatened through the usual peer pressure of the shopfloor Mafia to scupper any possible progress towards change. If we were not able to engage their minds in even talking about ways forward, then we would have to go back to the drawing board and search for other solutions.

The other, predictable problem was Baillie Fraser, the 'Back to Basics' man. Baillie always tried to keep any forward thinking back. He was uncomfortable with progress and fearful of the unknown, and we still did not know and could not explain where we were going. As a result, he sought solace in 'rubbishing' the project at every opportunity. 'H.G.V.' was not just a 'parasite', he was a 'f***ing parasite'... Fortunately, the others were quite used to this and those whose minds were rather less closed stopped up their ears with wax, or something. Peter Tait, the dyed-in-the-wool union man, was actually revelling in the debate, exploring all the obstacles with logic and calculation. The main group wanted the dissenters in, otherwise the whole thing would end up fragmented and messy. If the work force divided, the dissenters would have covered the shop floor in cynicism, encouraging a general return to the daily grind of work with which they were all familiar and – despite whatever spark of unfulfilled ambition may have lurked in their individual souls – comfortable.

You need plans...

I do not think I was much help at the time because I was grasping for abstractions, when the shopfloor men needed reassuring substance. I was finally persuaded to formulate a business plan after being told that, statistically, companies which have business plans perform better than those which don't. Why I was so reluctant to have a plan, I do not know. Maybe ultimately I am just a shopfloor man myself. During this time, 'H.G.V.' had introduced weekly sheets for the managers to write down their achievements and the issues they were planning to tackle. He also introduced a twilight meeting. This was a meeting at 4:30 p.m. after the day shift, at which we mainly used a flip chart to highlight information. It was a visible means of communication that enabled everyone in the factory to be aware of what was going on. It was good communication. The fact that there is good communication, of course, does not stop people complaining about how bad it is and my experience is that those who complain the most are the worst communicators, on a ratio of inverse proportion.

5

THE BUSINESS PLAN

The reasons why we needed a business plan were:-

- To stop us from stagnating;
- To overcome our lack of management talent;
- To develop and give scope to the work force.

I read books and borrowed other people's business plans to find out how to write a plan, all to no avail. The one spark of inspiration came from the management book, *Managing Change* by Bernard Burnes (Pitman) in which he uses the analogy of a lighthouse. In the dark you can see the light and the destination and although there are different ways of getting there, you can all see where you are going. This is the vision. The strategy is how to get there. I threw the books and other business plans away and wrote out the objectives that were pertinent to us and to us alone.

What we wanted from the plan was:
- To have in writing what is done and how we do it;
- To benefit the managers of the business in making the plan and referring to it;
- To be more professional;

- To facilitate succession;
- To aid/plan growth;
- To give us direction and a shared vision.

The other aid I found useful was K.P.M.G.'s, our accountants' booklet on business planning. This gives a structured approach which helps take the enormity and perplexity out of the process. I adapted this to our own needs and wrote out a series of discussion points covering such things as: business style; markets; competition; opportunities and future strategy. We also divided products & services and human resources into separate headings.

The trick, or the value of the plan, is to discuss it with everyone involved. I started talking to everyone in the company, four or five at a time.

How do you discuss the direction, the future, the succession and the role of the man on the shop floor if you do not really know where you are going? To remedy this, I crystallised my thoughts into a challenge. This was that I myself would get out in five years, whether it was voluntary or whether I was thrown out – the latter being the more hopeful course of events, because this would mean that the company would by then have developed capable management strong enough to throw me out.

The options for succeeding me were :

- Dynastic: i.e., passing it on in the family.

  I did not want this because I myself had been the recipient of nepotism and I wanted my children to lead their own lives without any shackles.

- Takeover: i.e., selling the company to an outsider and so ending the Main Tool as we knew it.

  This course of action, though endemic in industry, flew in the face of my sense of responsibility for the fate and future of the work force, and would by no means have guaranteed a future for the business.

- Milking it dry: i.e., taking all the money out through wages and pensions.

  This ultimately short-sighted course of action would have left the company chronically short of cash for investment and ultimately, resulted in liquidation.

- Succession: i.e., developing the people in the company to manage it into the new phase.

  This was my preferred option, but it was one that required an immense challenge to introduce new thinking, new ideas and a shared vision within the company: above all, with 'shopfloor man'.

I did toy with the novel idea of giving the company to the work force. They in turn would pay the family trust an annual sum in perpetuity. I proposed this to our accountants, who were somewhat perplexed as they had never heard of anything like it before. They quickly set out the ramifications and talked me out of my altruistic mood. It may be that accountants do not like moving out of their comfort zones either. Succession, statistically, has the biggest failure rate but this did not bother me as I relished the challenge, and I always had in mind the the back-stop solution, if need be, of buying in a manager.

Management by talking about...

Talking to four or five people at a time, I soon covered the whole work force. Nothing very enlightening came from this exercise, but it was still valuable in letting everyone know what was going on and what we were aiming for. It did, however, throw up an interesting discussion, not entirely relevant, with one group who all agreed that they enjoyed their work – apart from one worker who was adamant that he hated it and hated the company! The others, somewhat surprised, suggested that perhaps, in that case, he should leave? The person in question was our worst operator and, in truth, we would have been delighted if he had left. But he chose not to; and, despite his antipathetic attitude we kept him on, even though we did not have enough suitable work at his skill level to keep him busy. We did this because, at his age and with his skills, he would have had difficulty in finding another job. Yet despite this possibly rather rare outbreak of altruism in what has become a very tough world for employees, the man responded only with resentment. The best people know that they are good; the others only think they are.

6

CHARACTERS

Amid all the cut and thrust, pressures, confrontations and distractions of our everyday hectic working life, some characters stand out. One such was Jim Boland, our inspector and hammer thrower. Jim was big, genial and overweight. You could not meet a more genial and placid man, considering the turmoil and tragedy that seemed, quite unjustly, to befall his family. When the pressure became too much for him he would go crazy, lifting anything that was lying about and throwing it. People would scatter and, eventually, tentatively return to see if he had calmed down, which after a while he always did. My favourite Jim story, one that always makes me smile, concerns the time he went home and, after a hard day's work, nestled himself into his armchair. This was like a red rag to a – well, bull – for Mrs Jim who, half his size, nagged him incessantly for always sitting in his chair and doing nothing. She started. Jim, probably half expecting it, exploded. He stood up, lifted the armchair and threw it out the back door into the garden, 'Are ye happy now?' he demanded of the startled woman. After five minutes, he later told me, he had to go out and retrieve his chair because he had nowhere else to sit.

John McGregor was the man who would always 'tell you a better one than that', every time you tried to tell him anything. His previous company was next door to a fire station, which had a special tower for training. One lunchtime, John and colleagues went to watch a group of firemen practising throwing a dummy off the tower and catching it with one of those round, trampoline-like mats. According to John, they missed.

When someone tried to tell the lads the tale of how he'd had something stolen on holiday, John was quick to top his story with the (unbelievable) news that he'd had a pair of sandals stolen in an Arab country – while he was still wearing them!

One of his better ones from the shop floor told of a colleague on the night shift who was machining, on a vertical mill, a large and expensive casting. The company, Jig Bores Ltd., had a reputation for hiring and firing and so, when he machined too much off the casting, the man knew for sure that he would be sacked. For the rest of the night he worked like a beaver, sweat pouring off him, cutting and cutting the casting, until there was nothing left but swarf and a lot of cast iron dust. Next morning, when the foreman could not find the casting, he asked the operator where it was? 'But, I put it in a corner next to Inspection' protested the miller, innocently. Obviously, no one ever found it and he kept his job.

Another operator in the same machine shop was vertically milling a manifold block with a depth of cut of half a millimetre when the aggressive managing director caught site of it and insisted he should be taking a cut at least four millimetres deep. After a heated argument the operator put on a cut of four millimetres and nonchalantly told the managing director that that was the manifold scrapped as he was originally only taking a finishing cut.

Mat Brown, a toolmaker, was a small, bashful man with a speech impediment who was constantly teased by his fellow workers about his sexual prowess. Mat would always go along with all the preposterous stories told about him and, every 14th February, had a Valentine card in pride of place on his workbench. The sad thing is that it was always in his own handwriting.

He was always being made fun of and, when he bought a new combination lock for his tool box and had to memorise the combination, the others tried to convince him that he would never remember all those numbers. Mat, however, was wiser than they and not to be caught out. What he did was to write the combination on his bench, next to the lock. The sad thing is, he never could figure out how it was that the night shift were always using his tools...

Characters like these crop up in every machine shop and these are only a few among many. I think we have all met them. I am proud to number them among my friends.

Connel

The family holiday home in Connel, five miles from Oban, is where the business plan was discussed, at different times, with the top management and the charge hands. We had already subjected the top management to the indignities of psychometric tests, which they took obediently and failed (on a par with failing a urine test, I guess). At this time, our consultant, Lawrie 'H.G.V.' Spence, was still trying enthusiastically to push people into teams and generally make silk purses out of sows' ears. Fortunately for consultants, they only have to talk about direction and results. It is others who have the more difficult task of making it happen.

Our first meeting at Connel was with top management. The atmosphere, therefore, was tentative and not a little tense. 'H.G.V.' used Charles Handy's 'frog' analogy to get everyone in the mood for discussing – if not yet exactly actioning – cultural change. 'Frog' gives a somewhat slow motion, bludgeoning, subliminal message – thump it to the back of their heads even though they do not realise it. The frog in question is put into a pot of cold water on a cooker. As the heat is gradually increased, the frog first becomes comfortable, then somnolent, then soporific; and, as the heat intensifies, the frog, who has no longer any thoughts of jumping out, eventually boils to death.

This was a rather blatant attempt to finally ram home the message about not taking refuge in comfort zones and being reluctant to change. The management reaction was also predictable: humans, understandably, do not like to be classified with frogs. The effect of Professor Handy's story, sadly, is not to wave the magic wand and change us into princes... The result, if anything, was to stimulate further management obduracy and retrenchment.

So, nothing much revolutionary or even exciting happened with our personal development. But, in discussing our shared vision and the company strategy, allied to a review of the business plan, our new culture began to take shape. How we did things and where we were going had never been examined before in such detail, and just being able to focus on these issues away from the day to day operational concerns was a great help.

Part of the strategy was our commitment to go back into the manufacture of press tools, at which we had done well in the days when there was a market for totally mechanical products, such as typewriters. As electronics and digital systems took over, however, this market diminished; as a result, the subcontract supply of press tools dried up. Now that the computer industry was investing in O.E.M. (Original Equipment Manufacture), requiring a U.K. supply base, a certain demand for this type of tool could be clearly identified, and we were persuaded by our local development agency to provide the supply. As it happened, the O.E.M.s championed globally (to my mind, 'globalisation', with its madcap pursuit of the cheapest labour cost, is a euphemism for slavery) and the market dried up. Nevertheless, it gave us the opportunity to start on the road I had planned, to encourage individual growth and personal development. Raymond Davies, our best toolmaker, was elected to fulfil the role of tool room manager in that specialised market area.

On the shop floor, of course, the men were agog at what went on at our weekend retreat and now wanted part of the action. To me, this re-emphasised the lesson of the Hawthorn experiment; i.e., that in order to function fully, individuals need to feel involved. Our next move, therefore, was to invite all those charge hands who were willing to participate and go along with my theories to embark on a weekend at Connel.

Exploring the options

The format for Connel was a mix of formal sessions and more relaxed entertaining, where people could drop their natural reserve and let their hair down – those of us that still have any! However, the key to the success of a Connel weekend was to provide plenty of lubricant. We left work on Friday at 1p.m., arrived, started discussions – with beer – at 3:30p.m., finished at 7 p.m. and walked to the nearby hotel for dinner at 7:30 p.m. After this we walked back to the house to spend the rest of the night and half the morning drinking and talking business. On the Saturday morning we covered anything outstanding and I summed up. It was then back to the hotel for lunch before returning home.

To start the discussions with the charge hands I re-emphasised my vision by describing it as like seeing a lighthouse at night and trying to get to that lighthouse. There are different ways of getting there (strategy) but you still know where you are heading(direction).

After examining my own hopes and aspirations, and those of the family trust, I took them through the options for succession previously outlined – and the need to have a plan. I eliminated selling or milking the company, which left just the prospect of succession, either by nepotism or by developing the natural leaders within the company, at whatever level they might now be. The first option was obviously not attractive to me as I did not want any of my three children to feel compelled to come into the company, mainly because I myself had been a recipient of nepotism and did not feel comfortable with it. To me, the company at times felt like a ball and chain. I feel it is important that everyone should have the opportunity to find their own niche in life. You only have to look at the royal family to see the problems of children struggling to do their own thing under the pressure of tradition, in the glare of the media spotlight.

I am not sure at this stage what the charge hands thought of all this. It never ceases to amaze me, the number of times you can try to tell someone something and they just do not hear it. Unfortunately, I'm the same. I can only conclude that this is due to selective hearing; we listen only to what is relevant to our own situation and filter out the bigger picture. After all, you can only focus on and think about one thing at a time. I kept telling the charge hands it was not about money, and I wonder even to this day whether they could hear me, as they concentrated furiously on their own perspective.

The one charge hand who did listen, though, was our hardened Socialist reformer, the union man, Peter Tait. Although traditionally sceptical of management, he could imagine himself in my position doing the same. I found this interesting because to understand shopfloor man, I always put myself in the position of how he would feel and act accordingly with fairness and total conviction in any decision I have to make. It seemed he was doing the same.

So, what were the other charge hands to think? I was telling them that they had to play a more active part in running the company and become more managerial, but I was not telling them *how* to do this. I could have told them how by informing each one about the positive results that could be achieved by going along with my plan; but strong characters do not like being told, and it could all sound like so much pie-in-the-sky. I felt that if they were to develop they had to do so in their own way and in their own time and with their own ideas, for that measure of personal growth was intrinsic to the cultural change I was hoping for. We needed to have more people with ideas, initiative and even entrepreneurial skills. But these qualities could only come from the people concerned, not from me.

Halfway through our discussion, I took my courage in both hands and confessed that I wanted them eventually to run the company from the shop floor, because that was where it all happened. (Part of our philosophy was to maintain and nurture top skills because, nationally, the skill level was declining and if this was the case, we should always be able to find some way of selling our skills). I also told them that they were better than top management at making operational decisions, and so should not hold back from doing so just because they did not carry a title. I thought that would surprise them, but they surprised me instead by letting me know in no uncertain terms that they knew that already and why had it taken me so long to cotton on?

Although surprised, I thought this was a great thing to hear from them. It was now clear that they were not simply sheep, that although there was a long way to go yet, we could make progress in our development. It did, however, present one glaring problem – the continuing recalcitrance of top management, whom we will come back to.

We drank beer without restriction during the discussion but no one abused it and, if anything, I drank more than anyone. The charge hands, to their credit, seemed to appreciate how momentous the discussions could turn out to be, and wanted to keep their wits about them. Inevitably, there was some old ground to be gone over. After all, what other frame of reference did we have for a discussion of the future? Baillie Fraser saw to that. 'If we've been successful for thirty years, why bother with fuckin' stupid airy fairy ideas?' was his usual, trenchant response. And, surely, all you had to do was bring the work in and he would make a profit on it? It was like listening to a worn gramophone record, a 78... I argued eloquently that we were talking about the future, not the past; that the company had to change if it was to remain successful; that nothing lasts forever. Baillie stuck to his guns: it was as simple as getting back to basics. I tried to tell him that if the company stands still and does not grow it would move backwards by default because our competitors would not be interested in standing still and waiting for us to catch up. The argument, however, was to no avail: he still considered me an 'eejit', and there was no changing that.

The second main point I tried to get across to the charge hands was my realisation that you have to teach your men to be better than you in order for you to be better than them. It's the old angst about the privileges of rank creeping in, but I was now convinced of the value of this philosophy and the need to inculcate it in the company. Managers were there to manage, not to rule by divine right. Baillie's view was the antithesis of this because he always wanted to be the best, and to hell with the rest. I suspect also that his deeply traditionalist nature hid an authoritarian streak. The prospect of changing these 'best-worst' perceptions seemed nigh impossible, until at last, by some miracle of transference, Baillie found himself in a minority of one and was forced by the rest of the group to curb his natural negativity. With this positive peer pressure building up behind the plan, I felt that at last, I had seen the first evidence of a new management team forming.

Though the men had initially seemed apprehensive at the prospect of discussing these issues in the formal setting of a management seminar, they grew more relaxed and buoyant as dinner approached. I was probably the worst dressed person as, after wearing smart clothes all week, I generally like to dress down – tending towards the tramp look; whereas those who wore factory overalls all week were looking their smartest. Talk at the dinner table was easy and convivial to begin with, but surprisingly opened up some general philosophical discussions about motivation and happiness. Predictably, the men's argument was that money is the main driver in life, for they had not been exposed to the likes of Herzog, Maslow, McGregor and other behavioural gurus.

As a short cut, by-passing the behaviourists, I put it to them that if money was the great motivator, and I gave them twice as much, would they work twice as hard or twice as efficiently? This was a bit of a dirty trick to play on them. If the answer is yes, then why the hell were they only working to half their capacity now? I continued: 'Do football teams perform better because the players are paid more money? Did Paul Getty, one of the richest men in the world, work so effectively even after he reached retirement age because he needed the money? Does Bill Gates, head of Microsoft, conservatively worth over US$60 *billion*, go on doing it just for the money?'

These may be the most greedy people on earth but I doubt it. For them, money becomes an abstract thing which in turn becomes a measure of personal performance, no more. The real motivation is the challenge, the excitement and the fun of doing it. I wanted the charge hands to experience these ideas, and to their credit they listened.

Money talk was all-pervading and led on inevitably to happiness. To my disappointment (because I wanted an argument) they all agreed that money could not buy happiness. I was ready to steam into them and tear them to shreds, because this notion that happiness is an end in itself annoys the hell out of me. I become so worked up about it that it almost becomes an obsession, so I will pontificate on happiness elsewhere. Suffice to say that my view of happiness is that it is a great equaliser.

After dinner we meandered back to the house for a concentrated spell of drinking and talking. Tongues were loosened, and instead of free flowing debate, we got bile. Biles and biles of it. As a result, the hope that this would be our most productive session yet evaporated. We descended into an exorcism of people's hang-ups and how, the more hung-up they were, the more difficult it was to unhook them. To temper my disappointment I convinced myself somehow that, psychologically, this pointless discussion was good for them. At 3:00am, Baillie was the first to be carted off to bed, after which everyone gradually wandered off until the last, at about 6:30am, disappeared. As all the rooms were occupied, I got my sleeping bag out and settled down to get at least a couple of hours sleep when Baillie came in, sat down, and told me that it was time to get up.

Using work-study, I set up a production line to cook twelve fry-up breakfasts and with great pride served them all at one sitting. If I had to make breakfast for three or four it would have been a shambles; but, with a bit of planning and organisation, I did not have even one burst egg.

After breakfast, we summed up the weekend's events and covered any other business before walking over Connel bridge to have lunch and a pint before breaking up. My head was still nipping with all the activity and aggravation of the night before, and I felt somewhat deflated that we had not achieved more along our visionary way, with all our charge hands changed into forward thinking, educated and more than capable managers. Alas, life as we know is not that simple.

'H.G.V.' humoured me by convincing me that the exercise was not for my benefit but for our charge hands, and to that end I think it was successful. To lure them away from the work place, to get them to talk about their approach to their jobs, and to persuade them that they were actively participating in the way the company was and should be going must, in the end, be worthwhile.

Back at work, the shopfloor men naturally wanted to hear about all that had happened in Connel – while top management were equally curious to know what had gone on with the charge hands. I explained the gist of the weekend as best I could. I purposely did not take any minutes of the weekend because I wanted to keep it informal and we were not intent on specific functions but on growth and development. The shopfloor workers were intrigued; but when the opportunity later arose for the turners to go to Connel to discuss development and T.Q.M., they had more excuses than a bag of monkeys.

T.Q.M.

'H.G.V.', our consultant, talked to all the men in groups and had about as much success as I had warned him he might. T.Q.M., to my mind, is a management tool to try to make workers more responsible and to care; a shedding of responsibility, rather than a sharing of vision. It is probably necessary in organisations with semi-skilled or non-skilled workers, where the system is King; but our men are skilled, they have pride in the work they do and generally are their own biggest critics if the quality is not as good as it should be. In our firm, technical quality not a process that is amenable to systems management. As I had already told them in my introduction, T.Q.M. was not necessary for them because of the pride they had in their work, and this did not make things easier for 'H.G.V.'

What made the task ultimately impossible for the poor man was the rigid discipline and blinkered outlook, stemming from years of tradition, which goes hand-in-hand with this type of work. The 'shopfloor' culture had about reached its zenith in Main Tool at this time, and the men were ready for any diversion and sport, making T.Q.M. a plum target for the stirrers-up, and so it transpired. 'H.G.V.', shell-shocked, backed off.

7

THE SEARCH FOR GROWTH

About this time, we tried various projects to see if we could stimulate business growth and, possibly, explore new directions. Through the L.D.A. (Lanarkshire Development Agency) we foolishly spent money on visiting America, on trying to export to Europe and, most foolish of all, paying yet another consultant to try to identify a product which we could manufacture and call our own.

The L.D.A. convinced us somehow against all the best management advice that a product could be developed by looking at our resources and not at the market need, which would have been the more sensible way. After we had paid them the money, we were told that: 'Orifice plates and nozzles' were the coming thing, and felt even more foolish than before! Nevertheless, we were looking for the next step forward and with the help of the L.D.A. we bought ourselves another S.W.O.T. audit (we did so many strengths and weaknesses audits that it became a strength – or was it a weakness?) The government initiative gives you grants for consultants or training by consultants, but nothing for investment in the latest technology – indeed, the tax system works to encourage you to buy second-hand, which is hardly an advertisement for progress. I am convinced that the new acronym which should be introduced is T.Q.C. – Total Quality of life for Consultants.

The L.D.A. then approached us with their latest scheme – the tool making initiative. As we had fallen head first down every other hole, why should we not fall down this one? A group of tool making companies were summoned, to be told that unless we doubled our regional capacity in two years, the L.D.A. would have to bring in inward investment. This supply base, they said, was being demanded by the global O.E.M.s (big companies) in the computing and electronics industries, who needed tools for manufacturing components in the U.K.. Here was our biggest chance for years to go for growth – as well as give an opportunity to a charge hand!

Sons of the fathers

Raymond Davies was our obvious choice, and we made him the tool making manager. His responsibility for looking after our apprentices was passed to Baillie Fraser to enable Raymond to concentrate on press tools, on which he was eager and raring to go. So much so, that his complete tunnel vision on tool making and the success he hoped to make of it alarmed top management; for, their righteous argument was the patriotic one that you had to do it for the good of the company as a whole. It alarmed them even more when I sided with Raymond and insisted that tunnel vision was just what we needed. I believed, in a lofty but simplistic way, that unwavering determination has been, throughout history, the driving force behind the high achievers. I am sure that idiots also have the ability to be single-minded but Raymond is totally capable, quiet and reserved, until roused.

I was certain he was motivated enough, for he had to exorcise the ghost of his father who had been a company manager and a strong character. Although in our company we had previously experienced the sons of strong fathers, only to be disappointed by finding that they were the opposite of their parent, Raymond is a strong individual with plenty of tenacity. He would chew your leg off if you crossed him.

I also sided with him against top management in his choice of men he wanted in his section. If he was to be given departmental authority and not to be hindered by higher management making bad decisions, which would have lessened his chances of success; and, if we were to keep the management on their pedestal where they could knowingly shake their heads in mock commiseration with what they perceived as his inevitable mistakes, he would stand a better chance of success.

My constant plea to managers was to make subordinates better than themselves, so that they in turn would be better than their subordinates. This tended to fall on stony ground. From my own perspective, it was very much a desired outcome. The principle was clarity itself: if someone could earn twice as much money for the company as I could, then I could be humble and suffer by counting the money they made for the company. It would also thrill me to see such success. Surely, everyone wants the vicarious pleasure of their children succeeding and doing better than them. Then why not get that pleasure with your workers?

The earliest capital investment for the tool making was a wire erosion machine. The embryo for this technology was the humble spark plug, where the passing of an electrical current through a spark gap over time causes pitting and the wearing away of metal. Developing on from this observation has now given us the technology to cut hardened metal up to sixteen inches thick, without physically touching it, to any accuracy and shape you like by a continuous moving of electrically charged copper wire.

To acquire the machine, I selected three manufacturers with a pedigree, took two days over viewing their products and bought one on the third day. While visiting one of the factories, I came across a group of three people from one large company who had been in the process of selecting a machine for five months... I am sure that, in their corporate superiority, they probably scoffed at my naiveté in making an instant decision. But I was not there 'on expenses', I had a job to get on with. Management by intuition – the 'gut-feel' factor – is and has to be nurtured in a small company. It is more important to make a decision than to write a book about it.

8

REMOVING THE BLINKERS

Generally, our renegades wanted to be left alone. Being top skilled men, not having opportunities to grow and develop their responsibility, they see their mere ability as the pinnacle of their career achievement, a place where you stake your claim. Far from exploring the possibilities of managing and growing, and the additional personal satisfaction that might bring them, it seemed evident that they did not want any more responsibility. It showed, for instance, in their insistent attitude that all management had to do was bring in the work so that they could continue to get their 'two nights and a Sunday', as they had been doing all their working lives. Then they would produce and be content. Hardly a managerial perspective, it left everybody else with confused feelings of uncertainty and apprehension as what was to happen next.

Although we had abandoned the T.Q.M. programme, we still did not have a name for, or a clear-cut vision of, what we were trying to do. It did not help that our clever consultants and all the best management books were insisting that it was compulsory for successful companies to adopt a 'mission statement'... I was convinced that I did not need to bring out the rosary beads just yet. I preferred the airy- fairiness of what we were trying to do, as it seemed that from this less-directed course of action, something would emerge that was indigenous and unique to Main Tool. Until then, whatever 'it' was would remain nameless.

Bernard Shaw said: 'If you cannot change your mind you cannot expect to change anything.' I left a copy of this statement lying around, where our stuck-in-the-muds would 'accidentally' find it. I was still trying to win over a couple of dissenters who, by continuing to remain at arm's length from our plans for growth and development, would have brought us all back to square one. Much credit to the other charge hands, they perceived the important fact that we all had to go along for the ride, otherwise diversions and splits would render us useless. The frustrations were gnawing at me. The continuing uncertainties, the frequent knock-backs, the 'don't want to knows', the sceptics both on the shop floor and in management, were eating away at my resolve. I was trying to give these infuriating people decent opportunities, but they could not see this. My mental state had now progressed from anguish to 'why bloody well bother?'

Well, I will tell you why. I was playing God. I knew that what I was trying to do was good for them even though they did not know it themselves. I was more confident of their ability than they were, I loved the challenge of trying to make them see it, to awaken their latent ability and enthusiasm to grow their skills for the good of the company as a whole. I was convinced that, eventually, they would also enjoy the challenge – even though there would be no thanks for it, which I had no interest in anyway, and I would still be a 'conniving bastard' as far as my work force were concerned, forever afterwards. With each new setback, I should have felt a fresh sense of missionary altruism, of moral triumph. All I felt in fact was a burning desire to win – even if it meant giving them the bloody company!

New kid on the block

Jim Durnion, the new kid on the block, arrived like an angel sent from heaven. In fact, he arrived directly from Spain, where he had bought a bar, run it for one year, sold it and come back home. (It's a shame he's not writing this book instead of me. At least he could liven it up with a spicy account of sun, sea and sex – excitingly juxtaposed with a tale of machine tool minders in Strathclyde...)

It was all so matter of fact, though: Jim: owning a bar in Spain; playing lead guitar in a pop group; running a fabrication company... On paper, at least, it is hard to get your head around. What in the name of God was he doing in the Main Tool company? In practice, however, nothing seemed more natural. I could not make up my mind whether he was a latent entrepreneur, a winner or a loser. He was quiet, confident, good looking in a hippie sort of way, with a hangover sixties hair style; and one of these nice blokes you can't help envying. He also had ability and skill, and was almost immediately made charge hand of the tool making under Raymond Davies, whom we promoted to tool room manager. The only thing that worried me about Jim was that he was so helpful and obliging. I am not used to nice people, feeling more comfortable with oddball characters and head bangers. Jim was abnormal because he was so normal. Although his amenability was disarming he could fight his corner in an abstract and quiet way and win without anyone realising it. Jim had a secret that I wanted to find.

Jim was not only a Godsend, but he was like a job with a long feed. He gave us time. Time for staying calm and not making any irrevocable decisions we might have regretted later. Time to nurse things along, until the dissenters saw the positive side of our plans for development and growth and relaxed their hold on their comfort zone. They still needed to be convinced about the excitement of the challenge, like climbing a mountain. It is not being at the top which gives the pleasure so much as the effort and challenge of getting there.

Jim instinctively believed in what I was trying to do without being a Yes man (I tire very quickly of Yes men). Seeing the company with fresh eyes, his gratifying opinion of our skills and prospects was both a boost to me and a counter to the old hands. No matter what we did or tried to do for them, they had been steeped in cynicism for so long that their only-ever reaction was extreme suspicion and mistrust.What devious scheme was management up to now, apart from the axiomatic: 'trying to get them to do more work without having to pay them'?

It is a strange phenomenon that workers who have grown up in an organisation, no matter how good or highly skilled the work is, are generally derogative of their own company even though it is regarded in high esteem by an outsider. We had our fair share of these disparaging workers and not enough outsiders. Therefore, it was all the more welcoming to obtain positive attitudes.

The men were now hoping to play for time until things went back to normal and they could return to their mental comfort zones. Peter seemingly wanted to discuss it forever; while Davie and Jim, the progressive ones, were unfortunately in a weak bargaining position. It seemed like they were looking to the future, which is much less tangible than the past – that low mental ground from which Baillie would not budge – and hence, harder to sell the others. Davie would sigh in frustration outside when talking about Baillie's attitude, but he would sit quietly in meetings, biding his time. There are, as everyone knows, many ways of skinning a cat, and Davie eventually found one. Baillie soon became recognised throughout the company as 'The Dinosaur', and his section known as 'Jurassic Park'.

9

TRAINING

Our consultant, Lawrie 'H.G.V' Spence, as he was supposed to do, produced a training matrix for the company. Unfortunately, just as I had expected, it was completely useless to us. You can sometimes get carried away with government initiatives, management trends, the whole plethora of gobbledegook, ending in an orgy of avuncular pontification – in short, pure unadulterated crap... Just by way of an example, the Local Development Agency's budget is 90 per cent for training and 10 per cent for development. There is no need for training if there is no development.

If your top man earns the company £45 per hour and he can do that job better than anyone else in the country, it is preposterous to teach him to play the harp and send him on a 'Tom Peters'-type tour of the hotel conference rooms, so that he can learn to smile and be nice to customers. On the shop floor he has only the outlet of smiling and being nice to his machine. It is nonsense to train him for the sake of training him, there has to be a business gain.

What we were being subjected to was the formulated, bog-standard, Official Training Trap (O.T.T., definitely!). What we needed instead was a *training by-pass*, to avoid scholastic achievement which was irrelevant to our men and our company's needs. The intelligence was still there, only the formal schooling was lost and gone forever. The object, therefore, was to build on the skills and logic and experience of our charge hands, to open out their perspectives, enabling them to see the bigger picture. The purpose of the exercise was to give them the *opportunities* to use initiative, express their ideas and develop a more managerial and, (dare I say it?) entrepreneurial outlook. (No one said it was going to be easy!) You can't teach opportunity, you can only try to create it. Our training programme, therefore, was destined to be empirical.

Our first useless attempts at training were with top management. We peppered them with business books, extracts, epigrams and videos, all to no avail. They took refuge in the job they were doing, telling us and themselves how they were doing it for the good of the company. They retreated further into their shells, not wanting to be exposed, out of their comfort zones, in an arena where they might be seen and found wanting. They gleefully tore into us after watching a John Cleese video, where the main theme was the delegation of all unnecessary tasks. This may be practicable in a large company, they argued – but in a small company it would result in the pointlessness of the labourer doing all the work. Game and set to top management; but the match wasn't over yet.

Undeterred, we passed around titbits from selected books to some people whom we knew would make better use of them. Peter Tait and Davie McLaughlin were receptive and eager for knowledge, and did not have the hang-ups of top management or the fear of exposure. After the initial and favourable response, more books and thoughts were given to them,which were then passed on to the other charge hands. Only Baillie's predictable response, that they were 'a load of shit' and all you had to do was go back to basics, tempered the excitement of real progress we were making with the charge hands.

The next, and obvious, step was to send them to an introductory management training course. This was not so enthusiastically received, because they wanted to be paid for any time spent outside normal working hours. We settled on a day-release compromise enabling them to leave work at 2:00pm and take classes until 6:00pm. This lasted for about six weeks, during which they were introduced to management, leadership, motivation and other topics where they could genuinely and knowledgeably contribute. They lapped it up. For, apart from the learning and the debate, it enabled them to evaluate and criticise our own management. This was refreshing and encouraging because if management were not performing then it was negative and hypocritical not to look at any problems and fix them. We were now able to bring discussions up to the corporate plane.

The role of formal learning was now played down and the stumbling block of the 'mystique' of management was eliminated once and for all. At last, it had dawned on Shopfloor Man that management is all 'just common sense'. Hallelujah!

Training now had to become coaching; action learning, the master.. In Engineering, the most effective learning – and, to a lesser extent, in management – is achieved by doing. Even from university days, the thing I remember most vividly was participating in a management game where we were split into teams representing rival companies making a new product, 'Huckles'. After working out our costs we set a selling price of £7.50 for the 200-off huckles and waited to see how many we sold to the lecturer, who represented the market. We were delighted to sell all of our production of 200, until we discovered that one of our rival 'companies' was happily selling its huckles for £95 each! Totally perplexed, we re-examined everything; our company, our costs and our selling price, and went to the market for a second time, only to have the same thing happen again. Then it dawned on us: the demand was greater than the supply, hence people were willing to pay more money – we had not looked at the whole picture. That early business humiliation is an empirical experience that I will never forget, one that would not have merited much significance from reading about it in a book, or being told by a teacher.

An appropriate example at Main Tool was when Davie McLaughlin suggested a replacement to an old C.N.C. machine. What he did not look at was the economics involved. Although, undoubtedly, the £30,000 it would cost for the replacement machine would save us seconds on each job, we could not charge a higher hourly rate to pay for it, just because the machine was new; he was not looking at the potential of the £30,000 being used to buy something else which might give us an extra hourly charge-out rate as well as a time saving. Davie, to his credit, immediately accepted that he had missed a trick and would be wiser the next time.

To teach someone a task on the shop floor, you have to show him and then watch him perform the task correctly before you know he has understood it. It is sheer negligence, just telling him without this 'action learning'. It may appear to be overkill compared to the conventions of school education, the passing on of 'knowledge' in the classroom environment. It is a fact, however, that we only retain about 5 per cent of a 'chalk and talk'-type lesson. The fact that we have been doing it that way for hundreds of years does not validate the method. With 95 per cent of learning time wasted by not reinforcing lessons through practical experience, surely educationalists; or someone, somewhere, can do better?

10

SEEING THE LIGHT

The charge hands wanted another meeting. This in itself was tension ridden, because there is a traditional habit of informal communication in a small company and, unlike large companies, the overriding thought process in our company is that the work has to be done and not just talked about. Therefore we do not have meetings. Perhaps this is why talkers are more likely to succeed in larger companies, whereas small companies need doers. To the shopfloor men, it seems unfair that people are more impressed with talkers than doers.

Old Chinese saying:

'Man of words and not of deeds
Is like garden full of weeds.'

Symptomatic of this is to talk with great authority (does not matter if it is shite) and this will impress. Fortunately, with our charge hands it is sapiential authority that counts; an old play, *The Admirable Crichton* has an aristocratic family and their butler being marooned on a desert island where the butler has to take charge because he is the only one who can do anything practical. The very opposite of modern management theory, in fact.

This begs the question in large companies whether we are more comfortable being followers, and whether it is the cream or the scum which rises to the top. I've got my own opinion on that, too.

Anyway, the charge hands wanted to confront the issue of, firstly, what was in it for them and, secondly, what was this elusive 'personal development' all about? because, if this was something extra I wanted from them, then I would have to pay for it... The meeting had the confrontational feel of a wage negotiation. They wanted to have their wages consolidated into staff conditions before they would look at anything. They paraded the old chestnut about the unfairness of a sixteen year old girl starting in the office and being given better conditions than someone with twenty five years service who had put their life and soul into the company. This showed we did not trust them. Their arguments were eloquent, as they always are when they are looking for more money. They were allowed to rabbit on until I took all the tension out of the situation by agreeing with everything they said; however, it was a fact that being paid an hourly rate satisfied their earning power only through the awarding of overtime, and that tradition was the governing factor. The staff conditions they were looking for were given and accepted. I never, at any stage, did not trust them. Getting their preoccupation with this out of the way, we could now concentrate on moving forward. Were they now one of 'them'? Had their collars turned white overnight? What a blow for the socialist principle!

I had a list up my sleeve, of all the 'pluses' (remember my 'plus'?) they should now be encompassing. However, I did not tell them. For them to develop with initiative, it would have been counter-productive telling them, rather than letting them see for themselves the pluses they should be thinking about.

Unfortunately, no personal development was evident in the following weeks. We had not found the magic wand. One-to-one persuasion and coaching was in general giving us receptive ears without anything tangible in the way of people taking extra responsibility. In fact it was in sheer frustration with Baillie's negative attitude in particular, that I rushed back into my office, wrote down my feelings and frustrations on development, photocopied them and issued them to all the charge hands. This was the blunt stick:

Personal Development

- **Embodies new technology**
- **Interested in new ideas**
- **Ambitious**
- **Prepared to face new challenges**
- **Pleased to help and see others develop**
- **Keen to learn**
- **Learn from failure**
- **Want to know how to progress**
- **Prepared to be more exposed**

Personal Entrenchment

- **Fights against new technology**
- **Rubbishes new ideas**
- **Wants to preserve the old**
- **Jealous, hopes for failure in others**
- **Cannot be taught anything**
- **Fear of failure**
- **Only interested in money**
- **Does not want to move out of comfort zone**

I asked them all individually who I was talking about, and obviously no one wanted to see themselves under 'personal entrenchment'.

11

NEW DISCIPLES

Lolloping on to the scene at this time came Davie Semple, arms and legs flailing, with a tongue and a mind to match. If you were on the shop floor and big Davie came up behind you, you would have to walk faster in fear of him scuffing your heels. His ambition and keenness were on a par with his pace and voracious appetite for technology involving any new gizmo. He came to us, recommended by a competitor who had gone into liquidation, as a C.N.C. vertical miller.He soon proved himself and went on to programming the C.N.C. machines.

It was soon apparent that Davie devoured anything to do with computers and so he became our expert, writing software programs for estimating and parts listing. He was given the title of systems engineer, but was the type of character who could do almost anything well, e.g., operating a machine; programming; tool designing and anything else he was exposed to.

Davie was, intriguingly, two entirely separate people. For, along with his raw and eager talent, this rabid Rangers supporter was loud and coarse, unsophisticated and nervy, wild and untameable; an unbroken stallion. The Tasmanian devil was probably in a lower gear than Davie, and how to feed his raw energy was a problem. He was also the most agitated and vociferous adversary in our discussions about money having the ability to motivate; he was adamant that it did. Yet, in practice he was the antithesis of this in that you only had to dangle the latest gizmo or piece of technology in front of him and he was hooked. What do you do with a man like Davie?

Another person coming into the sanctum at this time was our Prince of Darkness, Stewart Miller. This materialised because of housekeeping.

My other vision, to brighten up conditions and make the work place a thing of beauty, was simply not happening through delegation to top management as the textbooks say it should. The initiatives and changes-by-example which I thought would have permeated into management and ultimately affected our stuck-in-the-mud culture, were scoffed at. The intellectual and artistic thoughts that were buzzing inside me were finally released by my son, Stephen, who was studying art at school and hoping to study architecture. During the summer holidays, he was brought in to do a bit of instructive labouring. This involved some painting of walls and floors. What he did was to paint a girder at the work place of a Celtic supporter in green and white stripes. Wee Pat, the Celtic supporter, loved it and was thought to cuddle it when no one was looking. Others then wanted customised columns as a result. For our visiting electrician who was known to take a dram, Stephen painted a wavy line along the floor to the electrics store, so that he could 'stay on the path'; I don't think the man even noticed! The initiative came to an abrupt end when he tried to paint our gruff storeman's fork lift pink. Stephen was told in no uncertain terms to f*** off, and did so.

What he did not get round to painting were any pictures to hang on the walls of the machine shop. That didn't happen until after a visit to Dublin where, after a few Guinness's, I bought some paintings from a student who had an exhibition in the pub. When we hung them on the shop floor they were tolerated with the customary sardonic amusement. But they were tolerated.

Continuing my good housekeeping quest, I proceeded in the way management books suggest, by example; picking up any rubbish and, in particular, oily rags which have the tendency to lie about and make the place look untidy. The overt show I was making was obviously noticed because one day, while putting on this performance, I was walking back up the shop floor when I saw some intermittently placed rags which I started picking up in anger, one after another, in a long line- until I realised I had followed this trail into the toilet. I had been 'had' but it still makes me smile when I think about it.

Stewart Miller now had this task of making the shop floor look good, special and unique with flair and inventiveness, without me telling him what I wanted. What would he do?

12

THE EMBRYONIC BUBBLE

We were now on the verge of breaking with the shop#floor tradition of the formative work ethic: too much respect for authority and power. I did not want the men to swing back into their comfort zone of cynicism and resentment within the working class, stereotyped, Presbyterian work culture.

Any residue of resentment and resistance would cause unrest, fearfully taking us two steps backwards – especially with Baillie, who still would not budge an inch. There were others too, who had authority in name only. But real managerial authority was not something, after the years of distrust, that they aspired to or were comfortable with. Shopfloor Man personified the working mans' ethic, with his strong belief in the power of work; hard work; making money; sacrificing for the family; doing your best; giving unending loyalty and deferring constantly, grudgingly to authority. These were all-too prevalent and too much bred in the bone for him to accept easily the passing of traditional authority and power. It was now vital that Baillie and his ilk did not sway the group into retrenchment. Continued momentum and forward thinking were imperative.

Another meeting was needed to give them direction and to allow them to question my ideas. There was no tension now, so no one need be on their guard.

Growing the bubbles

An hierarchical chain of command was drawn up to look at where people were in the organisation. I circled their individual positions a few times for emphasis and called it a bubble, because it looked like one. They now had the authority and responsibility, so if their bubble grew and created £1 million sales for the company it would rise to the top, and top management would be subservient to the bubble blower.

Knowing them to be normally a bunch of cutthroat mercenaries when it came to the assumption of additional duties and responsibilities, I suggested that the rewards for growing the bubble would of course be commensurate with the success. They astonished me with their reply, 'No, it shouldn't. The money gets used to grow the other bubbles.'

It wasn't until sometime after the meeting, talking to them individually about their journey into this uncertain world, that I noticed they kept referring to the 'Bubble theory'. And so it was born.

13

TEAMWORK

Rarely have I seen such massive brainwashing and heard so many hackneyed platitudes as I have with this concept of 'teamwork'. Inevitably, people will say, 'It's all about teamwork, right?' and we all nod our heads and condescendingly agree, 'Yeah, that's right, teamwork!'. I'm sorry, but that's just what it's *not* all about!

Have a team by all means, if you have work for a team. If you don't, then forget it. How is a team useful for a man working a lathe all his life? (and please don't say the inevitable, that the whole company is a team. It is not. It is an organisation with multifarious complexities and pluralism inherent in it, and is no more a team than a friendly society of masochists and sadists, which may, in fact, be a better frame of reference for a company. It may be time for a preservation society against teamwork and exponents of teamwork).

It sometimes feels like I am fighting a lost cause, but fight it I will. I want people to develop with ideas, initiative and forward thinking. I would love them to fly. To be shackled to the ball and chain that is the team, tempering their drive and entrepreneurial spirit, subordinating themselves to the irrelevancies of the 'group' mentality, such that no individual dares or is able to stand up and be counted when necessary, is frightening in its intellectual implications. If God had wanted us to be sheep, he'd have given us fleeces.

The first exposure I had to teamwork, which probably marked me for life, was in primary school music class where we were put into team rows and given points for good behaviour. The intellectual arrogance of a poncy primary school teacher treating streetwise kids like that was diabolical. In reply we all competed by being so chaotic that we would be awarded the lowest points. That teacher deserved all he got. Maybe he went on to be a consultant.

Okay, a team can work and possibly contribute more than an individual by the simple fact that you have more minds to call upon and, therefore, more ideas and more options than just one mind. But deciding whose ideas are worth more than any other member of the team's is nigh impossible, if the overriding concern is to keep the team united. And the mind of a trained team member is, by definition, less capable of creating and developing original ideas, since all his thinking is of others. If, however, you have a large group or a mob you can have a tendency towards chaos or a lynch mob decision.

Teamwork, or to put it in a more common sense way, free from the overload of the mantra status of the word, the ability to work co-operatively when the need arises, is undoubtedly important and, indeed, imperative for many projects. Coming back to specifics, as our charge hands do not have any project-based work, but function mainly using their own initiative as individuals, then they have to utilise any latent skills at teamwork in another way.

Using teamwork without teams is perfectly feasible and sensible. Our management and charge hands all had their team profiles taken. This was done by a questionnaire which resulted in everyone knowing what their characteristics were, pertinent to a team and also knowing the characteristics of others.

These team elements were developed by Dr. Meredith Belbin at Cambridge university and with my explanations are :-

The SHAPER – breeches in and gets things going and makes things happen.

The IMPLEMENTER – can follow and implement.

The RESOURCER – like James Garner in the film, 'The Great Escape'- obtaining passports, clothes and stuff.

The PLANT – the ideas man, he can be creatively disruptive and frequently collapses meetings, but seldom leads from the front.

The FINISHER – dotting the I's and crossing the T's.

The CO-ORDINATOR – organises tasks and who's doing them.

The TEAMWORKER – smoothes arguments to keep the team working as a team.

The MONITOR – assesses what is happening and what has happened.

After having your profile done, it is fascinating to see how extraordinarily accurate it is. So much so that it is able to withstand any disbelief or cynicism from its detractors.

The trick now, is to know what you and others are good and bad at. You should not worry too much about your deficiencies, because all you have to do is call upon a colleague who is good at that particular thing at which you are bad; e.g., if you are hopeless at form filling, call upon a 'finisher' who loves filling forms and thus avoid putting yourself through agonies and wasting time. Give someone else that pleasure.

Along with team profiles, we did the supplementary psychometric testing which highlights personality characteristics such as tough-mindedness and extrovertedness. (It was pleasing to see what I had expected; i.e., that the charge hands were predominately shapers with tough-mindedness. These were the characteristics best suited to satisfying our managerial objectives of personal development and growth.) They were no longer wary of these exposures after the precedent at their introductory managerial course where they were taught the different styles of leadership and profiles.

They were in general genuinely open and interested in their profiles, except for Baillie, who constantly wanted to know how well he had done and if he had passed... With all the interest generated, it was time for another Connel.

14

CONNEL AGAIN

The weekend was set for more discourse, discussion and development. I went through all the things I wanted them to do and what I wanted them to think; all those lofty thoughts about taking authority, responsibility and initiative, so that they could experience the fun and the thrill of management. My preparation was exhaustive, but I was still not happy with the content. There was too much 'me' in it.The obvious dawned on me, that it was counterproductive if I had to keep telling them how to have initiative. I decided that I would do the introduction to the meeting and then walk out, leaving the rest up to them.

At the meeting everyone settled in at the table with their cans of beer and chocolate biscuits, expecting the usual argy-bargy about all aspects of the business. This would quickly have deteriorated into another comfort zone, discussing what had been and what was; as, having been part of it, you had the knowledge to talk with authority. To talk about what was *going to happen* in the future demanded more ideas and more brain power. Inevitably, they would grab at the comforting, known past rather than try to crystal ball gaze the frightening, unknown future.

So, I started on the past and where they had been a year ago; tied to a machine tool with the same prospects for the next twenty years. I proceeded to ask them if they all understood my vision of the Bubble theory. No one was in any doubt about what I was trying to achieve. They did not, however, have any conviction of the next step for them and no inkling of their own vision. This was the pinnacle of my frustration because reaching this point with our development and theory I had imagined this would have been the watershed. A case of go forth and multiply – except now it seemed as if it would be fifty-forth. At this point I proclaimed that I had achieved my objective of finding the key to job enrichment by giving them more scope and opportunity. It was up to them now. I lifted my can of beer, said cheers, and walked out.

Apoplexy is too strong a word for the reaction as I walked out, but astonishment and disbelief were momentarily obvious at my performance which, I must admit, I thoroughly enjoyed. It was no abdication of my duties or any washing of hands but a calculated gamble that they would take up the challenge and continue without me.

This, after they recovered, they did. Peter Tait was well versed in holding meetings and so continued with my written agenda. I do not know what went on, but I could imagine myself cringing at them not being more visionary but delighting at them being so intelligent. We never did take minutes at any of our meetings and I say that provocatively because professionals always take minutes. For us there was no need because what we were trying to do was more on a spiritual level, not governed by a timetable or placed in a straight-jacket of things we had to do. It was *the culture* we were working on, not a project.

As they came out of their meeting, the roles were reversed. They were cock-a-hoop and confident, while I was pensive and unsure; although pleased that my gamble to leave it to them seemed to have proved successful.

Excitement and confidence were in the air as we walked down to the hotel for dinner. The main course was a choice of steak or salmon. The B.S.E. crisis having exploded in the media the previous day, the hotel manageress was apprehensive about offering us steak. She should not been. We ordered ten steaks and no salmon. Once a shopfloor man, always a shopfloor man – nae class.

Back at the house, with a coal fire and a plenteous supply of malt whisky, I anticipated a loosening of tongues and possibly a productive topic and discussion. The opposite happened. It turned putrid with all the built up angst and petty frustration spewing out like a friendly venom. The only way to think of it is like a vile tasting medicine – it must be doing you good. Whether it is exorcising pent-up emotions or whether it is just too much consumption of whisky, I do not know. Fortunately the evening did not end with any real malice and we happily went to bed.

About 8:30 the next morning, I was making everyone's breakfast when Baillie hobbled in to the kitchen, on the way to the toilet, wearing only white Y-fronts. He stalked me into a corner and spluttered, 'Well?', prodding himself on his chest with both straight fingered hands. I could not understand the question, but I was a bit concerned as it seemed serious. 'Well?', he asked again to my complete bemusement . He put me out of my mental anguish by hitting me with the full statement : 'Well? No bad for a man of fifty-five, no bad'. 'Naw, no bad Baillie', I agreed – for a man with arthritic knees, an asthmatic chest and piles. He then hobbled happily to the toilet and I continued making breakfast.

After breakfast I was invited back to the summing up of the proceedings. It was established what each person's next step forward should be in creating and growing their bubble. It was gratifying that no one was happy with their lot as they were on stony ground and we did not have set guidelines to help them. Everyone also appreciated that they were all different in nature and had different functions and were being encouraged to find their own level without any comparison to anyone else. It was up to them.

We now had our customary twenty minutes' walk over Connel bridge to have lunch. Baillie disappeared as we were commenting on the idyllic setting looking over the Falls of Lora and the lovely view down the Oban coastline to Mull. He came back after ten minutes to explain, as only Baillie could, how he had shed his load and the effect this had on his piles. Amidst all the excitement of progress and the aesthetic delights of the West Coast, this was Baillie's living metaphor of going back to basics. Would he never change?

15

THE MAN FROM GALILEE

Not Jesus. Not the man who had so many notches on his gun, but the man who tormented my mind in the garden of Gethsemeny.

Stef Werheimer is a modern day Robert Owen. An enlightened, visionary industrialist, he exports over £90 million a year from the highest hilltop in Galilee. To call his empire world class is to discredit him. Who is this man who impressed me more than the man from Nazareth, and what is he talking about?

His tool cutting company, Iscar, in its marketing and public relations, invites customers to a free trip to Israel to visit his creation. Apart from the opportunity to visit the country, I was more intrigued by the man and his achievements.

The company occupies a whole industrial estate, with ultra-modern factories equipped with the best and latest machinery, run mainly by robots. Stemming from this, it has beautiful landscaped gardens with sports facilities, interspersed with magnificent sculptures. It also has an art museum, a vintage car museum, a primary school, a university and a new town within a couple of miles, with all the most up-to-date amenities you can imagine.

The primary school, which is also open to people not working for Iscar, teaches Hebrew, maths – and then anything else the children want to learn. The business community founded its own university, to focus on the needs of engineering education that other universities fail to meet. The students work five twelve-hour days; three at university and two at the company. There is a plastic mould tool subsidiary run and worked as a fully commercial operation by students, for the learning experience. Another fantastic concept is Stef Werheimer's incubator factory units, which he lets out to fledgling start-up companies with central administration and canteen facilities. They are allowed to stay for five years to establish themselves, after which they are forced to leave and go it alone. The mutual benefit is them feeding off Iscar and Iscar having ancillary and competitive services on its doorstep. What a concept!

Stef's inspiration and vision is for countries in the middle east to create other industrial estates in this image and likeness. This to him would be the means to stability and peace in the region, where neighbouring countries could use their energies to create wealth and a higher quality of life and social structure. – Wow!!

They come from all over the world to the east to see this star. John Major, Gorbachov, Kissinger, Arab leaders and a host of influential power brokers and politicians, all come to admire, bringing gifts, then ignore everything they have seen. For seemingly, it has changed nothing. The politicians and power-brokers do not believe in what they see, even though they can touch it, smell it and taste it too. They are wary of people with vision; and, after all, although not a carpenter, isn't Werheimer just a shopfloor man at heart?

We constantly hear the gripes of business leaders about the importance of manufacturing industry, and how politicians are just not interested. It is perfectly understandable therefore, that if politicians come from the academic world, research and suchlike, or the so-called professions – most are lawyers – then they are not going to be comfortable with manufacturing and hope that it goes away. We in manufacturing would be exactly the same if we were in power. We would not think that the academics and lawyers produced much wealth for the country, or were of much value.

My Garden of Gethsemeny

After the visit and back at our small hotel, I immediately went down to the hotel garden, reneging on a nights drinking with the other lads, for I had been exposed at Iscar to more then I could mentally absorb.

The garden was in semi-darkness and empty as I sat alone with my head buzzing and nipping. My thoughts were in turmoil. I was plainly disturbed enough to cause some of the lads to come out to enquire if I was all right?

What was I doing, snatching these people out of their comfort zones, playing God, shaking them to their mental foundations and turning their lives upside down, with all the fear and anxiety that had provoked, just for a business experiment? Slotted neatly into the Protestant work ethic and tradition, bred for generations in the service of traditional manufacturing industry, they knew the rules and accepted them, happy enough to be the worker and provider for their families. They knew, or thought they knew, exactly where they fitted into the hierarchical authority of the work place; they were stubborn as mules in their resistance to any interference with that. They knew their place, or thought they knew it, even in today's rapidly-changing world – where those traditional working class values and loyalties can easily be imagined to have been swept away by a great draught of deregulation and social change. But have they? These all-too human beings were apparently content with being a 'shopfloor man' to their dying day, and fiercely, proudly resistant to anyone who wanted to change them. Who was I to sweep away everything they stood for, and were most familiar with? You can't live other people's lives for them.

My 'business plan' required that they had to change their mind sets from taking refuge always in blaming management for all their ills, to taking responsibility for their own personal and career development. Did they even understand what those hollow buzz words meant? Is there not an 'up side' to this total deference to management? Yes, it can result in a lot of grumbling and barracking and cynical resistance to initiatives. On the other hand, it is an intense expression of loyalty to the company. It is really a question of shifting the patterns, of getting them to transfer their dependence from the authority of a few managers, to the interests of the company as a whole;and further, to then recognise the dependence of the company on its external markets. Such a simple notion, but how to achieve such a dramatic transformation in people who, like recalcitrant children, simply stopped up their ears and did not want to hear the message, thinking it synonymous, presumably, with nasty medicine? The only way to increase their effectiveness and to get them wanting new goals was to stimulate the internal process of questioning and change. But it was not up to me to do that. They must want to take up the challenge. They had to climb the mountain for themselves.

Then, what chaos would this process engineering trigger within the company, where a lower tier of management was unprecedentedly being told to run the business in preference to top management? Not as a game, to be played on some time-honoured anniversary, All Fools Day perhaps – but for real, for ever? What added pressure and resentment would be brought to bear on the charge hands by top management, should they perceive that their power base had been drastically eroded? Did we even need top management any longer? And how much cynicism would be generated on the shop floor, with the predictable sneer, 'aye, now it's all chiefs and no Indians'... Would the men appreciate that the new culture offered them more opportunity for self-advancement, and that their interests lay in 'growing their bubble', so that the company's bubble could grow in total? Or would they continue to see it as a management plot, a 'get rich quick' scheme at their expense?

Could it all be kept in control? Was I going to be crucified? Was my conscience clear?

A myriad of questions, but no solutions. Stef Werheimer's tremendous achievements and vision had not sprung into being fully formed, but were transitional and embryonic in nature. Big things from small beginnings. At every stage of this miraculous transition he has wrought, new conflicts had to be resolved and new visions adopted. These transitions and challenges would doubtless have tortured him with impossible conundrums, no more nor less than they were now tormenting me. It was only a matter of degree. If this was the case, then it followed that the charge hands were being equally tormented and again it was only a question of degree. If in terms of our spiritual evolution we are all on different planes, as I believe, is it not incumbent upon those above, to elevate those beneath? Maybe it was time for what the Americans call 'tough love'...

My time in the garden was, I knew, vitally important. I had to make sense and order out of the potential chaos I had initiated back home, and absorb what I had been exposed to here in this extraordinary frontier society of relentless energy, perpetually unresolved conflicts and unbounded possibilities. Surely, the 21st century is being hammered out here? My overwhelming feelings of self-doubt were already fading, for I had seen the light. I was Saul on the road to Damascus. I saw the apparition and I believed.

My reeling mind was cemented firmly back in my head. My resolve was strengthened. I was not going to be crucified after all, so I went to bed and slept.

16

REFLECTIONS

After Jerusalem, it was back to basics (mine, not Baillie's). Central to my conviction that what I was doing was the right thing was the obvious fact that, unless we did something, we would not have a chance of achieving success. Our quest for aspiring to become 'world class' was abandoned. Scottish class – first class – would do for now.

Not for us the latest management fad of striving for 'world class' like every other go-ahead company, pushed like lemmings over the edge by the propaganda from consultants subsidising their cushy lifestyle with ever more improbable and costly 'solutions' to 'problems' of their own inventing. What did 'world class' mean? We would never be really big, like a G.K.N. or a Babcock. We would never, literally, conquer the world. That sort of rhetoric is for consumer brand managers.We could share some of the values of 'world class' – service, customer orientation, quality, on-time delivery. Innovation, yes to an extent; although major innovations now come almost exclusively from expensively-funded research institutes. And we were undoubtedly committed to the interests of our work force, unlike those who merely pay lip service to the notion of 'investing in people' while they are busy 'outplacing' them. But 'world class'? It sounds like a complete con for a small business, in a small island! Why anyone spends good money going along with it, I cannot think. Perhaps we are all lost souls, terrified of change, seeking any lifeline through the minefield of the future.

No, we wanted something else for ourselves. We wanted to be *unique*: an often-expressed, but more often derided sentiment.

If a fingerprint is unique, to my simple mind, a person must be unique; and we have some crackers on the shop floor who have virtually cornered the market. Isn't it more interesting to promote and encourage this uniqueness as an organising principle, however chaotic – rather than squash it, as large companies have the tendency to do, with their vast 'human resource' departments, by pigeonholing their employees into their own comfort zone? (Incidentally, did you read that report from the good old U.S. of A. that showed company performance tending to move in inverse proportion to the numbers of H.R. specialists employed?) Industrial life would be more colourful if we had more barmpots and no less effective if they were capable barmpots. It would create a more fertile source for ideas – a genuine 'human resource', not just an expensive packaging of consultancy values.

Generating ideas is excruciatingly difficult for we mere mortals. Try locking yourself away in solitude and thought, with the sole purpose of being creative and coming out with some brilliant ideas – or even halfway good ideas, only to find that your brain is not as clever as it is supposed to be. In fact, it does not even appear to belong to you, for it will seldom produce thoughts to order. Granted, we are conditioned as children and have our minds disciplined by an educational process where wrought learning is the dominant philosophy – well, that's my excuse for having a mind cast in cement. But it should never be too late to change. Then, why should we change or want to change, unless we perceive it to be in our best interests to do so? And that requires a capacity for abstract thought...

The need to want to change has to be there because there is only one person capable of achieving it. I cannot change for you. It can, however, be stimulated, prodded or bludgeoned into being. With the charge hands, the possibility of change, the idea that it could happen, was titivated by the judicious feeding out of enlightened extracts from selected books and videos on the subject; then prodded along by face to face discussion, argument and persuasion – but never bludgeoned by the threat of 'change, or else...'. People respond to coaxing and the promise of immediate rewards, not to threats and abuse, or 'jam tomorrow'. 'Change, or else...' may be a quicker method, but by convention and, hopefully, wisdom, not the best method, as it produces the wrong kind of change, the kind you don't want if you can avoid it.

Apart from the gifted and high achievers, then, those who already have vision and imagination, change is hard work for the vast majority of us. There has to be something in it for us, otherwise the change itself is the threat. The rewards can be the excitement and thrill of doing something you have never done before or never thought you could do but always wanted to. The challenge and sense of achievement, the breaking out of a humdrum life and boring existence. The chance that you may become a better person with more opportunities. The buzz of doing something creative. The sheer enjoyment and the flashing by of otherwise dull time wasted in monotonous endeavour. But I'm getting carried away on this tide of change!

It would be nice to let your mind frolic naked in the park; dance into the unknown; into the clouds or, if it's already there, back to earth and to hell with the esoteric.

Give your brain a twirl of Russian roulette. Stretch it; test it; confuse it; outsmart it, and then, you too could become a barmpot. You too could have ideas and inventions. You too could discover perpetual motion. You too could become a genius. You too could be a daft eejit/ off your chump/ a fruit and nut case!

17

BUBBLE THEORY

After all our developmental worries and mental anguish, the Bubble theory could now be set in stone, if you can have such a thing as a stone bubble.

Figure 1

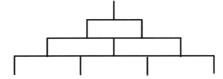

Figure 2

Organisational standard hierarchical structure (figure 1) is adopted by large companies and is a hand-me-down from the armed forces. In practice, it can become too rigid and too cumbersome, creating internal politicking and jockeying for positioning within the chain of command, with too much time and energy squandered in bureaucracy.

If the war analogy has to be used then the Bubble theory (figure 2) is pure guerrilla warfare. Devised, more-or-less, by the Romans, figure 1 has taken two thousand years to arrive at. Figure 2 took me only two years.

Getting back to figure 2, the three-pronged right represents the company secretary, company development manager and the managerial director. This is the engine for company growth:

Company Secretary = financial control, budgeting, support and teaching of commercial awareness.

Development Manager = can be called upon by the bubble blowers for growth in sales and market direction.

Managing Director = kicks in with ideas, suggestions, direction, coaching, teaching, encouragement, criticism if necessary and protection from the 'knockers'.

The three-pronged left represents:

Works Manager = makes sure the processes on the shop floor run smoothly.

Technical Director = nurtures customers by estimating and servicing them to their satisfaction and beyond and then passes on the appropriate customers to the bubble blowers.

Production Director = focuses on production control, efficiency and quality.

And that, basically, covers our ideal management model.

The horizontal line is there in print only. In reality, it is an invisible line (the shortest distance linking two points) which can easily be broken through by the bubbles as they grow and rise (circles in figure). With no impenetrable tiers of 'boxes' above, the field is clear for the bubbles to develop and grow – doing it their way, at their own pace, with whatever they need to succeed: luck, the right environment, market demand, the necessary drive and determination. The opportunity and the potential for growth and development have been created by the removal of the hierarchy.

By moving the top management to the sidelines in a more supportive and servicing role, the breakthrough by the bubbles is not only more feasible but much more focused. No longer do the bubble blowers have to move up the chain of command for promotion for it has been removed. The only promotion available to them is the self-promotion involved in growing their own bubbles until they break through the line. 'White Mercs for all', as we like to say (although we don't mean it:for all their mercenary instincts, our charge hands at Main Tool are savvy enough to know that reinvestment is the key to profitable growth and job security.)

They have to run their bubbles as owners would in their own businesses. They have to care. They have to become 'Bloody hell!' men. When mistakes are made and problems arise they must have enough concern to say, 'Bloody hell!' and do something about it – unlike larger organisations where the 'Bloody hell!' man can disappear and be lost or even deliberately buried in the self-seeking chain of command. They now have the responsibility, the authority (why do so many managers imagine you can have the one without the other?) and, above all, the opportunity to care – and the vision to see why it makes a difference.

The contention that people are the most important asset becomes more than just lip service. It now becomes a challenge in stark reality. They may not have the entrepreneur's greed for money and all the worldly and envied trappings it may buy, or be in the right place at the right time; but they still have the intelligence and, hopefully, the will to win. Now, they also have the opportunity.

As the bubble prospers and grows it creates opportunities through growth which can be used to start other bubbles, giving opportunities to other developing and capable people. It should perpetuate growth, and the 'chain of command' hierarchy would still be eliminated: as the bubbles expand and grow, the horizontal line simply expands to make more room.

Here are the hard facts of the Bubble theory:

- It encourages individual growth.
- It facilitates company growth.
- It removes the threat to top management.
- It gives closer communication with customers.
- It creates job enrichment.
- It gives the effect of running one's own business.
- It creates entrepreneurial spirit.
- It flattens the structure. (to keep management gurus happy)
- It's more fun.
- It's unique.

It's also now recognised management theory. A recent article by Alf Young, Economics Editor of our national newspaper, the Glasgow Herald, proclaimed: 'Bubble theory is more than froth' and went on to devote twelve hundred well-chosen words to the history and development of the company, how I came to be running it, why I wanted to change it – and, above all, how my instinctive, home-grown thinking on the subject of creating opportunities for the employees in order to boost profits for the company is 'in the emerging intellectual mainstream' of management theory in the U.S.A.

As the Bubbles start to rise

During this period, Raymond Davies was progressing with his tool making Bubble. For twenty years he had worked at his 'trade' (staff people don't do real work). Now, not only was he putting on clean hands, but he was starting to explore the virgin territory of his own personal feelings and emotions. In addition, he would have to find, cost, price and profit from work obtained on his own initiative. It was no longer 'management's' job to go out and get it. The job of tool room manager did not exist until then, there was no precedent or role model for him to follow or emulate. He did have a desk, which he kept moving about to create space – but no office. This was not the best way to make him feel secure or confident, but that was not what I wanted in any case. Not to begin with..

For a time he moved about from man to man and job to job trying to feel busy, occasionally helping out as he weaned himself off a lifetime of manual work. This limbo was soul destroying. He wanted so much to prove himself, but found that there was nothing he could get his teeth into. He was starting off with zero market share. All eyes were on him; he had no tools to shape this thing with. What was he supposed to do?

In retrospect, I still haven't a clue. I am afraid he was destined to make his own way through this transitional period. It probably caused him a lot of personal suffering.What I did do was try and teach him things from my own experience. How to estimate quickly and efficiently, simplifying the process and taking out the mystique. He quickly learned how to find the cost of a job, but then had to find the guile in pricing it, because cost and price are different quantities. He had to learn: how much he could charge customers without them becoming unhappy; how desperate the customer was to place the order; what competition he had and how much they were likely to charge; how to say No, in order to avoid the trap of taking on work that would not pay, to the exclusion of better paying work (any fool can be busy with work that does not pay).

Raymond had to learn how to think on his feet, how to see the bigger picture. Many others' managerial tools and techniques were passed onto him. This learning process helped occupy him until the work started coming in and his engineering skills and knowledge could be utilised, proving that the faith and trust bestowed upon him were justified. Once this fear of not fulfilling his expectations was gone, he became a happy man again. We all have twinges of self-doubt at times, but it takes only that first measure of success to dispel them.

Raymond inherited the ownership of the tool making before our Bubble theory was developed; and, although his promotion was of a fairly conventional sort, it became the forerunner – though not the frame of reference – for all the other Bubbles. Raymond was always on the periphery of our quest to develop the charge hands; but he remained independent and single-minded, and this was ideal for our objective of creating the individual 'in his own image'. Initially uncertain of our theorising, he was nevertheless extremely useful as a critic in the positive sense; and was open to, and supportive of, the idea of giving others opportunity. As he moved into the office to deal with customers, the timing was opportune, for it allowed Jim Durnion to step into our theoretical model by taking ownership of the tool room for himself, and claiming it as his Bubble.

18

MORE PROGRESS

The market opportunity we had been hoping for conveniently arrived with the increase in oil-related work. The oil industry demands immediate response, and our years of traditional thinking that on-time delivery is not imperative ran contrary to their 'just-in-time' culture. Overcoming this problem created the perfect opportunity to generate a bubble to channel focus on delivery and service, mainly in turned components which covered about 90 per cent of our oil work. Davie McLaughlin, our turning charge hand, was given this responsibility, with the remit of supplying a quality and service that our customers could not do without, thereby gradually increasing this market and edging out our competitors.

Davie's transition in coming off the machine and becoming more managerial was faster than Raymond's. He now has responsibility for a bubble of 14 people, with the power to hire and fire them without my say-so. Whether all our talk of change or learning from Raymond helped this process did not matter as it quickly paid dividends. His first thoughtful action was to group similar parts together, facilitating more efficient production. He was also helped by being given all the necessary figures, enabling him to measure the work and become more commercially aware. It is unbelievable to think now, but this would not have happened before. The data would have remained fiercely in the possession of 'senior management', doled out like sweeties to the deserving children. In fact, it was all too easy for David because he was still too comfortable. He was sleeping too easily at night – 'Let me have men about me who are lean and hungry', says Brutus. Well, he's not exactly that. He was capable of being pushed further, though, and I needed to see and feel evidence of his anxiety before I could accept that he was out of his comfort zone and hence, more fertile for change and development.

I started teasing David about visiting Aberdeen and meeting our customers to understand their needs and to hustle for more work. He was warned not to rely on other people bringing work in for him; as, to satisfy our theory, he had to become more influential and entrepreneurial. As the work potential increased, he was even questioned on strategic issues: what machine tool investment should we be looking at to increase our market share?

To test him out, our technical director advocated spending £200,000 on a specialised lathe that no one else yet had. David thought this was a great idea and the only way forward, until I pointed out that this kind of work covered only 5 per cent of our market and maybe there were better opportunities in the remaining 95 per cent? The question of return on investment was put to him: should he buy two, three or four machines or even used machines? It must be a daunting task for anyone in his position to be faced with these new predicaments. He soon became anxious, which pleased me because now he was thinking more. Now, he was ready for development.

The rate of change

It constantly surprises me that bright people whom you would imagine to be most receptive to change can often be the most stubborn. An example from personal experience is the head psychologist I know, who is hopeless with people. Constant attempts by her subordinates to get her to understand people on any but the most cerebral level have failed. In our own work, we have top management whose brightness cannot be questioned. Yet they are fearful of having their brightness and performance measured in any way, perhaps being reminded of their school days. The opposite case, again from our work place, is our C.N.C. turner who painted an abstract modern art masterpiece which now hangs on our shop floor. For him, this was a totally new experience, a genuine process of opening up the flaps on the advent calendar and discovering new and delicious nuggets of creativity within. Change is not all about profits on the balance sheet.

Character, as earlier discussed, can be measured by profiling and psychometric testing. It may be sheer personality, however, that can create openness and desire for change; also the will to win. I have my own wee formula for determining the rate of change in any organisation:

$$R = \frac{BC^2}{2E}$$

Where R = rate of change, B = Brightness, C = Character and E = Environment. (Environment is important: consider that, while 90 per cent of the children from a residential area in the Home Counties will invariably go on to university, from an area like Bellshill, where I come from, the intake is around 2 per cent.)

However, Character is more important: it's what gets you out of your environment, so that's why it's squared. (I'm now trying to build in a parameter that stands for Native Resistance to Change.)

When using this formula, by the way, don't forget to add on the idea you first thought of. The other thing the theory tells us is that engineers should stick to engineering... Management consultancy is not my line!

A thing of beauty

Why should the shop floor not be a thing of beauty? To spend most of your working life in the one place, it would appear to be sensible to have it clean and bright rather than to come in every morning to be greeted by the legacy from the traditional grimy industrial past: grey, dirty and dull.

This was one of the running arguments I had with Baillie who thought that, with his skills, it was more manly to produce good work in difficult conditions. It gave him more pride being able to perform in a shit-hole. The bigger the shit-hole, the more proud he was. A clean and attractive place of work was not for him – that was for 'poofs'...

Trying to convince Baillie was pointless but it was imperative that I should not let dinosaurs rule. The effort and show I had gone in for, of picking up loose, oily rags, had only a limited effect in trying to get the work force to 'think clean'. A bolder move was to hang up large paintings of abstract modern art on the shop floor, much to the bemusement of the work force. After the initial perplexity, it was gratifying to see how quickly they accepted it. Almost to the point of demanding, why shouldn't they be part of something special? I may be wrong, but I had the feeling that they appreciated the fact that I thought highly enough of them to know that they too were comfortable with, and could aspire to, the higher things in life.

The only negative turned into a massive positive. Tommy, our C.N.C. turner and resident cynic, said it was a 'f***ing load of shite', and that 'anybody could do shite like that!'. He was taken aback when I agreed with him and then did the dirty by asking him to do one himself. This was not as subversive as it appears, because Tommy had hit on an underlying truth in his deep philosophy and erudition. 'Anybody' could indeed do that... I have always wanted to believe that it isn't necessary to be a great or famous artist to produce beauty and that there is merit and integrity in honest toil – as opposed to the affectation and arrogance which emanates from and is all pervasive in the art world. I so much wanted Tommy to succeed.

Succeed he did, and we now have his large work of art hanging proudly on the shop floor. In my opinion, it's the best. Its uniqueness is more genuine due to the fact that he has never painted anything in his life before, or even looked at a painting with any sympathy; and so has created something completely free of any subconscious influences. The painting was featured, along with my photograph, in an article on the company in The Herald, our national newspaper. But it was Tommy who was the more proud, and I secretly envy him. He has something he has produced from his own imagination being admired by all, while the rest of us are still sitting in our own comfort zones, muttering: 'Sure, anybody could do that'.

19

A GIANT LEAP FOR MANKIND

Led by the Prince of Darkness, Stewart Miller, our Service bubble now gave more options for improved housekeeping. He had more focus and ideas than top management because he applied himself spiritedly to the task. Quickly and quietly, he organised the non-productive workers in stores, cleaning and dispatch. Whether it was persuasion or fear, they did what he asked. But then, they knew he was capable. The bottle neck, otherwise known as The Inspection, was similarly well organised, with the disciplines of quality taken through inspection to paperwork and packaging.

The shop floor became noticeably cleaner; while something else Stewart did was both a breakthrough and a turning point, to my mind, in all we had been trying to do.

I came into work one Monday morning and found all the protective boards around the machines which had previously been a dull green colour, painted in multi-coloured, abstract designs. Everyone different. Yah, beauty! my mind shouted. Here at last was someone with ideas, using initiative. Not only was it a breakthrough, but it livened up the workshop; which, although much cleaner than before, was still a bit insipid. I thought it was wonderful. Even if I had hated it I would have told Stewart that it was wonderful because wonderful it was to me, even though top management didn't like it.

Drawing inspiration from my enthusiasm, and perhaps remembering my son Stephen's earlier efforts at painting the girders in Celtic colours, Stewart proceeded to paint theme boards. For our old soldier he painted camouflage. For our musician, a sax; for our angler; a pole; for our golfer, a hole. He organised our reception area to be painted with a coat of arms, utilising men who had run out of work. He was given the job specification of doing anything he liked, provided it was *different*. Top management had previously been given this task, with the reminder that management was running the system 'plus', and that *making a difference* was one of the 'plusses'. The best they had managed, however, was to suggest that the reception area could show photographs of some of the work we do, just like every other boring company in the world. To my mind, this was the very antithesis of the type of thinking we had to encourage. (You may well ask, gentle reader, why I have not fired the lot of them by now...I suppose they have their uses; and besides, as I have already said, I am as resistant to change as the next man. But watch out!)

Stewart not only had the bottle to do something different and imaginative, but he had the cheek to have cartoons painted on the wall, which I was a bit dubious about but accepted because it was the men's own work. The rotten pig kept me in this state of dubiety by continually asking me what I thought of them, before calling his own bluff – explaining patiently that it was only a joke and they would be painted over. The Prince of Darkness did not mention this to anyone else, and neither did I, until the hostility and pressure from top management reached fever pitch. They even went to the trouble of soliciting comments from our customers that it was hardly the proper thing for a company with our image. Eventually, the cartoons were painted over.

This pyrrhic victory for top management was perturbing. Did their astonishing hostility to the men's cartoons mask their true feelings? How solid was their faith in our vision? Did they secretly imagine that second tier management were becoming too powerful and a threat to their security? Did they fear that, in the coming revolution, aristocratic heads might roll? Were they just hoping to hang on until the Bubbles burst?

It was doom and gloom time again at Main Tool.

Gloom at the top

Everything that seemed to have gone in our favour was against us whenever top management were involved. Their cold indifference and animal cunning were evident from their instinctive efforts at self-preservation. They staked their claim in the iconoclastic nonsense that they were 'doing it for the company'. To me, this was childish and infuriating.Every time they repeated this mantra, I knew in my heart that it meant they were doing it for themselves. But they had found their fervent defence and, like fanatics, believed in it fundamentally.

It was George Bernard Shaw who said: 'Patriotism is the refuge of the coward'. Oscar Wilde put it more strongly as: '...the last refuge of the scoundrel'. In company life, the noisy expression of patriotic sentiment invariably stands for self-preservation and stubborn resistance to delegation and the imagined loss of authority that comes with inevitable change. True patriots just get on with it, they don't sit around prevaricating, or worry about where the next onyx table lamp is coming from.

If their rug is being pulled from under them, where should they stand? Unfortunately, they did not embrace change when it was offered and so Hell mend them. Actually, violence is no solution, only an emotional outburst, for which I hope I can be forgiven. Of course, you can't resolve management conflicts like the kiddies do in their computer games, however tempting it might be. You can't just zap someone who's in-your-face annoying you with their illogical intractability, and hope to fill the space with someone more congenial. At this precise moment I am sitting with my elbows on the desk, holding my head up by its face, because I simply cannot resolve the problem. For a start, whose problem is it – theirs or mine? I want them to come to me with solutions, not problems and so I should go to them with solutions, not ultimatums.

First of all – the problem:

- They complain about communication and yet will not communicate.

- They insist that it is all about team work and yet will not play in the team.
- They say that they want to learn and yet will take no courses and read no books.
- They work long hours to prove their loyalty and yet will not do anything to improve efficiency.
- They say that they will help everyone and yet will undermine anyone.
- They say that they are doing it for the good of the company, but transparently operate to their own agenda.

Apart from being totally non-supportive, the main tactics of top management can be categorised as Direct and Indirect.

Direct = Blame shifting. Blaming the charge hands for such things as quality and production control errors when they themselves were entirely responsible.

Indirect = Subversive propaganda. Telling others that our development of the charge hands was not working and should be scrapped. (They were doing this for the good of the company, you understand.)

There was only one way to counter these tactics, and that was to confront them head on. I told both the charge hands and management exactly what was happening, and why. My aim was to stop any further erosion of our vision and to flush out any hidden agendas. Management were cornered into showing evidence of their commitment to the process. Admittedly, their authority was being dissipated by the Bubble theory. With the flatter hierarchical structure we now had in place, I explained, their role was now to be supporting, coaching and advising – helping others to grow, instead of blocking and, ultimately, upholding their tutelage.

Somewhere here was the solution. If our theory succeeds – and there is still no reason why it should not – then individuals will make it succeed. If any charge hand's success can be attributed to top management then top management can take the acclaim and the glory. They should become wise uncles, guides and councillors; and find merit and honour in this noble aim. Isn't that a better epitaph for a manager, 'he helped others to get on in life', than: 'his missus has a unique collection of onyx table lamps'?

20

EMPOWERMENT

We now had an organisation without a recognisable structure. The chain of command was loose and erratic. The charge hands were still exploring their parameters. Some more than others, because we do not have any guidelines or measurements, it's up to them where they take it. Top management were slowly coming to terms with the fact that their illusions of grandeur should be finally dispelled.

Most important of all, however, sales and profits were making rapid advances: the extraordinary thing about this process of turning the business on its head, and making the managers manage, instead of obstructing everything, is that it works. (Others have found this out too – read Ken Lewis' seminal book on How to Change Your Company and Enjoy It! - Management Books 2000).

Customers, consultants and commentators say we are practising 'empowerment'. Perhaps that's what we're doing, but I have not caught up with the latest jargon. I am still stuck at 'job enrichment', a conceptual problem which manufacturing industry failed to solve twenty years ago, and which I am still striving to solve. When I do, I will jump two decades of solving nothing and clatter with empowerment – a word I hate. It makes me cringe. It is a frightening, ugly, in-your-face, authoritarian neologism devised by management consultants to create an illusion of industrial democracy and New Age thinking, merging under the guise of social progress. It seeps out of Harvard through academics and is advocated by modern American managerial convention. It is wrong. It works, but it is wrong.

'Empowerment' is wrong because it is based on a premise which was as wrong twenty years ago as it is today and is as insulting to the working man. For, wriggling about beneath the wonderfully optimistic idea that organisations should be all about devolving power and encouraging people at the lowest levels to take responsibility for their own decisions (that other unlovely word, 'subsidiarity', springs to mind here), are those inevitable management consultancy snakes-in-the-grass – measurement and money.

We are told to fix everything so that it can be measured and reward accordingly. This is a switch on the old idea of the rat race, so disparaged by social commentators – you had to rush around like a rat, and work hard to make money. Well, doesn't that sound better than rushing around twice as fast, achieving 'performance rewards' which can be translated into 'shareholder value'? For whose performance? And what are you getting paid in the meantime? It seems to me, the old rat was at least relatively free in his sewer; today's rat is trapped in some ghastly lab experiment. Who loses, when you gain? Are you even allowed to care any more? Successful entrepreneurs, individuals who are single-mindedly focused on making money to the exclusion of all other human values, are now our role models. The moral philosophy here is on a shaky nail. If there is no finer thing on this earth than money, then it's time to give up. This idea that because money can buy everything, it is everything, to me seems the ultimate symbol of a society in terminal decline. If 'empowerment' is only really about maximising shareholder value, if it is about the 'greening of power', then give me job enrichment every time.

Enrichment is so much warmer and more inviting, and such a *nice* word... To develop for altruistic reasons is no more easy than converting every value into a numerical equivalent, but much more beneficial to society. In order to make better money, rather than building for aesthetic reasons, and on a human scale, the unfortunate architect has to design buildings which are such abominations that they have to be pulled down. Good for the developer, he gets a second bite at the cherry. Money as a driver for all actions must be suspect. In a recorded test case, psychologists gave teenagers of equal ability the challenge of walking a tightrope. Without letting the others know, they offered half of the group a sum of money if they succeeded. The ones who were not offered the money generally performed better. They only had to focus on the challenge and enjoy that challenge, whereas the others were diverted with thoughts of money and fell off the tightrope.

To have money as the bottom line in your life is to diminish the objective, and the intrinsic value, of doing a good job to the best of your ability and for your own esteem and respect. To participate in a company, it is still more important to do something because it is right, rather than because of the money. We should make allowance for honest integrity, where someone works hard and tries his best even though he is not perhaps as effective as a money maker who is of dubious character. The true profit lies elsewhere. A shopfloor man should be able to lay claim to being an essential part of the company's structure by the good he does, and the way he enhances both his work and his own self-esteem, rather than measuring his success by the size of his wage packet. To be frank, it would never be big enough. This is particularly important in the company with a high level of skills and a long training period. The short-term, hire 'em and fire 'em accounting mentality of certain companies may bring paper rewards, but at the expense of their souls. And companies *do* have souls.

The shopfloor man wants to enjoy his work. He wants to do a good job for a fair wage, for himself and his company. Certainly, he wants security but he also needs recognition and trust and responds to it. Treat him fairly and he also will be fair. Generally, he is enthusiastic and so we have to feed that enthusiasm. He does not need control but guidance. He wants his company to be successful and so we have to find ways of helping him to contribute to that success. He is not a donkey who needs the carrot of money. This is what job enrichment is about.

This is the basis on which our Bubble theory was built and the rationale behind the development of the charge hands. In turn, they will have to help in solving the problem of job enrichment for the shopfloor man, chained to a machine tool. This next, logical phase of the process presents a challenge which still has to be faced.

Progress report

To keep the continuity of the Bubble theory going, a meeting with the charge hands was called for. The cold, confrontational meetings of the past were gone and so now we could look forward to mutual trust and an openness which encouraged people to say what they thought, no matter how raw boned.

After the usual flak aimed at Baillie, something he enjoys because of his desire for being the centre of attention, we proceeded with the meeting. It did not throw up any surprises. Our prospects for work were promising. Opportunities to work in closer partnerships with customers were becoming more realistic, mainly because our larger customers were being sold on partnership by their consultants and beginning to believe in it and act upon it and not just talk about it. We were now in a better position to make it happen. We were psychologically attuned to the idea of customer-focus, and had the management and project engineering potential to take advantage of any opportunity. With the company prospects out of the way, we came to what they wanted to hear: their own progress reports. It is always reassuring to note that people are more interested in themselves than anything or anyone else.

The mid-term reports were read out without discussion so that no one could hog the limelight. The bare headlines read:

Stewart Miller – Started off with a bang. Going steady and doing a good job but needs to be revived to move forward.
Peter Tait – Looking for and needing a spring board.
Jim Good – Doing everything that was expected of him and more.
Jim Durnion – Quietly and competently working away but needs to expand. Should help to move **Raymond Davies** on to greater things.

David Semple – Still trying to satisfy his enthusiasm and energy.
Baillie Fraser – Holding his ground.
Davie McLaughlin – Doing a good overall job and advancing man-
    agerially very quickly. Needs to do something about man to man
    confrontation which he appears to be afraid of.

My own mid-term report was written down as: 'Still apparently
leaving things to chance and not giving enough direction'. What I
actually said was: 'Doing brilliantly as usual'. This did not get the
reaction it deserved – the men only laughed.

Surprisingly, no one complained about their report; but pent-up
emotions were released, and someone lashed out about how hard he
had to work in comparison to some other charge hands. He wanted an
answer to: 'How the fuck am I slogging my guts out when there are
bastards doing bugger all?' (eloquence was not one of his strong
points). Peter Tait, knowing full well that the comment was directed
at him, asked him in a calm and dignified manner, knowing well what
the answer would be, just whom he meant by that? Receiving a
straightforward reply, Peter's admirably restrained response was that
he was carrying out his new role with every bit as much dedication as
his accuser, and did he not trust to that? The man replied that he did
not. As Chairman, I felt it might be time to intervene.

I started to explain that Peter, in his own time, was designing and
producing a company brochure. But Peter Tait was proud of his
honesty and felt no need to prove himself to anybody. He was also
somewhat peeved that I should have to defend him, which he was
more than capable of doing himself. Perhaps he was making it seem
too easy. Others could not see the pressure he was subjected to and the
hard work he was putting in. Like most of us when we are working
hard and someone accuses us of not pulling our weight, he became
annoyed and resentful.

I think it also surprised the other charge hands that management
was supporting not only a noted trade unionist with old-fashioned
socialist principles, but someone who also apparently was not
contributing to the spirit of the Bubble theory. A further explanation
was needed and given, as I explained Peter's situation. His was the

smallest bubble, and he was under some pressure, given the understanding that someone else would eventually take over his vertical milling section, which comprised only three men. He should have been the one who was resentful; he was the one who, more than anyone, appreciated the Bubble theory and the opportunity inherent in it; he, more than anyone, was prepared to move out of his comfort zone and try new things. The challenge now was to find him something he could latch on to, in order to prove the theory.

It was agreed that there should be more communication to prevent internal emotions and resentments boiling up. For a bit of fun, I told them I had a new vision. After the chorus of 'Oh, no!', I told them my new vision was to be named Businessman of the Year. This was the proverbial sticking the toe into boiling water... But there were no laughs. In fact, their reaction was surprisingly supportive, as they showed no apparent doubt that I could achieve this lofty goal. They did not ask about the procedural rules, or whether it was the Businessman of the Year in the whole country or just in the Main Tool company but instead, accepted the fact that it could happen and that they, as I told them, would get all the reflected glory because it would be them that made it happen.

They only warned me that 'when' (surprisingly when, not if) it did happen, they would make damn' sure I remained down to earth.

I don't know why I suggested this idea of being Businessman of the Year (it hasn't happened yet!), it came off the top of my head and on reflection I can only wonder whether this frustrated desire for recognition is part of my shadow side, where I am subconsciously looking for reward. Jung or Freud, I am sure, would have postulated that it was a substitute for not receiving sufficient praise from my parents as a child, and having this overwhelming desire to prove myself. I would like to postulate further and say that every man needs to achieve great acclaim, before he can show how humble he truly is.

Is this in itself not narcissistic pride? Is this the hidden shadow I have not seen?

Sinclair on buyers

I have always thought it an oddity of business life that buyers, by and large, have such a distaste for associating with sellers, and vice versa. You would think they would get on together, having a mutual interest in exchanging goods and services, oiling the wheels of industry, and so on; but the fact is, they can't stand the sight of each other and meet as infrequently as their bulging diaries (and now, God help us, their voice mail) will allow.

I suppose the difference is that, while salesmen tend to be cheery extroverts, interested in making and spending a bob or two, buyers are brooding introverts whose only thrill in life is to scrape a penny. Although this observation is generally true, it does not lessen the interest in looking at the methods of buyers. It was important that the charge hands, if they were to be successful business developers, should become wise to their nefarious ways. An awareness, therefore, of their styles, as opposed to dealing in actual personalities, was essential. To recognise the style enables you to be more enlightened in the pricing and bargaining game.

The 'screw you' buyer

The 'screw you' type is the most easily recognisable. He knows you can't do the job for the price he wants and is prepared and is at ease with himself that you will lose money at his price. He justifies this to himself because he does not 'force' anyone to take the job on. His tactics can include offering you the job as a favour: 'It's yours if you want it'. The desire for work if you're not busy clouds your intelligence and stimulates your greed. You take the job and discover that any fool can be busy with work which does not pay. Another tactic would be to put out ten or more quotations to catch the ignorant, the weak or the people who will make mistakes. The way to deal with this buyer is easy. You reciprocate the 'screw you' philosophy by suggesting that you will not 'force' him to buy at his price either, and leave him in the shambles he will inevitably create and deserve by going to the cheapest possible competitor. Then, you should look for the companies with buyers who are more enlightened and more professional.

The 'knock it off' buyer

My favourite type is the buyer who, after asking for your best price, insists on knocking something off for good measure. This is done more often than not in a friendly and playful manner. Elaborating patiently on all the reasons why you cannot lower the price any further gives him his opportunity for his favourite line about getting the hanky out. If his fix is getting a reduction then give him the thrill this time, but add on 10 per cent to all future quotes. The reason I like him so much is that sometimes he forgets to ask for a reduction.

The 'half price' buyer

The buyer that puzzles and amuses me is the one who can always get the job done elsewhere at half your price. It is puzzling, because you wonder why he is sitting in your office, rather than passing the time of day at the half price place? It can be amusing when, if you quote £400 and he tells you that he can get it for £200 from a competitor, you suggest politely that he buys it from the competitor? Invariably, you find out that the competitor can't do it in the time, or to the spec., or in the colour required. The last time I dealt with this situation I capitulated and told him if I wasn't doing it my price would be half my competitors at only £100. He thought that was a great price. I had to remind him, however, that it was only on condition that we did not get the job. He still thought it was a great price. Sometimes it is a waste of your time trying to be too clever with people for whom money has become a total substitute for reality.

The 'friendly' buyer

The most effective buyer is not the straight-as-an-arrow, three quote man taking the lowest price without communication or influence but quite the opposite. This clever, cunning devil is your friend. Yes, he follows the procedure of obtaining three quotations but then assures you with moist eyes that he really *wants* you to have the job if you will only do it for just under your competitor's price. So, not only does he obtain a price lower than the lowest but he selects the one he thinks is the most suitable company to do the job. It was quite a time before it dawned on me that this type of buyer was much smarter than I was, because he was doing the same with our competitors...

The 'bully-boy' buyer

The bully-boy is generally the buyer from the large company on which you depend for a substantial slice of your order book; although to them, it is just peanuts. Assuming all the majesty and financial clout of that company, he cajoles and threatens you to accept jobs with impossible deadlines and prices, much against your will. The opposite reaction to this patent abuse of his position is to make him pay by unashamedly taking any opportunity to get even. Letting his tyres down in the car park is a temptation... Or, you could remind him that his Accounts department still owes you for the last six months' deliveries.

Variations on a theme

Although variations of buying techniques occur, it is not all one-sided. Sellers can also have their devious ways. It was a competitor in fact who let me in on the secret of how to quote a price on a rush job. He starts by telling the buyer that it will cost, say, £900. After the buyer nearly faints, he quickly offers him a better price of £300, at which the buyer is delighted. After all, has he not saved £600? The job is only worth £90, yet the buyer is happy! Although this scenario is extreme it nevertheless exposes a hidden principle in buying and selling, which is never an exact science. It is that *you charge as much as you can without making the buyer unhappy*. However, the overriding credo must always be 'a fair price for a fair job'.If anyone is playing unfair, the invariable rule must be: keep your dignity and walk away. You'll be amazed at what turns up the next day.

21

FORMAL COMMUNICATION

The charge hands agreed to meet me on Monday mornings with our weekly sheets, summarising what we had done during the past week, what issues had to be discussed and what we were going to do that week. All the charge hands, that is, except for Stewart Miller, who was too busy and in any case always tries to be uncommunicative, and Baillie Fraser – who insisted, not surprisingly, that all you had to do was bring the work into him and he would make it pay. It was the nail in the coffin for Baillie's development and for Baillie himself. After the years of self-aggrandisement, negativity and criticism it was sad to realise that he had in fact no capacity for openness, that he was ready for the dinosaurs' graveyard. It was unfair to try and force him out of his cave, we all knew.

Stewart Miller's refusal was not a negative to me because I knew he wanted to progress, but without the soft, namby pamby way of having to show up for meetings when there were more important things like work to be done. He always excused himself by saying he was too busy. Although reticent and uninterested in these joint discussions, he seemed more appreciative and understanding when given information privately. I therefore made the habit of going to see him while he was working to communicate the key points I had discussed with the others.

On one occasion, a comment of his bordered on surrealism. I had to think twice, when he said he did not have the luxury of time to think and that it was fine for me because I had nothing to do anyway, (he was more correct than he realised). Because I had nothing to do, I suggested that I could perhaps think for him- a proposition to which he surprisingly agreed. I then put my mind to his situation and generated a list of his thoughts and ideas. He thanked me for them and did not disagree with any, except that he knew what he was getting for dinner that night and did not need me to think about it for him!

These weekly sheets were often judgmental. Peter Tait was verbally eloquent, gained from years of indoctrination in the Union; but he could not apply this to his writing. Davie McLaughlin was supportive. Davy Semple was erratic and often did not stay long enough to discuss anything but was intent on running out and telling everyone. Jim Durnion was an enigma. He could not write; he was not articulate and yet he seemed to get his message across by some inborn telepathy that needed no words. I invited Baillie Fraser to come in without having to do a sheet, but he never did.

I did not know what to expect when we initiated the ritual and I was happy to pre-empt their sheets by having no expectations and excluding any thought of what might be written on them I had painstakingly told them that I deplored hidden agendas and they could be as frank and open as they liked. In response, Jim Good was questioning, thought provoking and knowledgeable.

Creating vision

Davie McLaughlin's wishy-washiness and lack of intent and aggression was annoying me. He was still too complacent, too understanding and too comfortable. To eliminate my frustration, and to try and get him more focused and case-hardened, I wrote out a sheet of questions that I wanted answers to. I wanted him to think and take ownership of questions such as:

- Where do you see yourself in five years?
- What is your vision?
- How are you to achieve that vision?
- How big do you want your bubble to grow?
- What improvements can be made?
- How do you give your men job enrichment?
- Why do you not want your own balance sheet?
- How much work have you brought in?
- How many customers are you talking to?
- What are you doing about efficiency?
- Why are you not improving your machine layout?
- Why are top management doing your work for you?
- Are you estimating? If not, why not?
- Why is housekeeping around the lathes so poor?
- What makes your service better than competitors?
- Why are you not doing more work with existing customers?

This was only a selection of the questions I put to Davie. And they were pretty tough ones to answer. His answer on receiving them was somewhat predictable: "Oh, shit!'. Nevertheless, after two weeks of prompting he came back with an answer to every question. Not wanting the exercise to fritter into the obscurity of time, I used his answers to write out a personal development plan, which would give him something tangible to aim at. I was determined that Davie should not wallow in his comfort zone, because he was much more capable than that – even if he didn't know it yet.

The charge hands had to develop like the mercurial vision, they had to know what they were trying to achieve. It was my responsibility to guide them when I myself did not know the answers. Fortunately, I could give them the questions and that was half the battle or, realistically, one eighth. They needed guidance in what was expected of them and in what they had to do to achieve it. If they were entrepreneurs, they would have done it themselves by now. Indeed, they might even have been telling me how to do it. As it was, they had to learn from me. Not quite a case of the blind leading the blind, so much as 'the untenably self-deprecating giving wisdom and guidance to the uninitiated'; mine was a position in life I had neither aspired to nor desired, being basically a fellow-cynic.

What were the unknowns, obvious to me with my longer experience, that would most effectively help in the learning process? How to pass on useful *experience* – which is so much more important than formal, academic management education, from which no real learning can ever result? I could not teach them gut feel, no matter how good I thought I was at it. The weekly sheets were the nearest answer. I could write down my issues and thoughts and explain them on a one-to-one basis to the charge hands. Hopefully, experience would be short-circuited and, presumptuously, they would learn from me... At least it would make them think.

I decided to do my weekly sheets, not in a contrived teaching format but in a day-to-day, run-of-the-mill, working mode. Even if I did not do things professionally they would still learn something by criticism or default – although I was conscious of stretching them somewhat. The problem was that I did not know, and still do not know, how effective this process was or would be. It was another case of trying one's best, without the superior knowledge or hindsight which gives you the confidence to believe that what you are doing is right.

Self-motivation

We used the same sheet for all the charge hands. Fortunately, the others wanted to hear explanations of any provocative remarks and emotive ideas expressed. Hopefully, these would get through to them and underline our philosophy and culture – as well as making them think. They were still stuck with the basic business of shaping metal to turn a penny; but they were also stepping up to look at life on a different plane, which not many of us have the opportunity or encouragement to do. Normally, you have to do it for yourself.

Self-motivation is, inevitably, a necessary part of dragging yourself up the ladder without anyone to encourage you. With all the motivation we gave to the charge hands, would it not be reasonable to expect them to succeed in casting off their ten, twenty, or thirty years of being shackled to a machine? I wanted them to learn, in a short space of time, the things it had taken me twenty years to learn. I could not gauge my influence on them, so how could I influence and help them? It was a dilemma. My decision eventually was to stay true to myself, not to try to play to their level. If I knew wholeheartedly that I was being honest with myself and them, it avoided the necessity of playing games. Truthfulness and integrity are no bad ingredients with which to blend any culture. If you are not a complete smart arse, I recommend you try it.

Critic, counsellor, consultant...

Apart from running the company, in essence, what I was doing was being critic, counsellor and consultant, all rolled into one. Although I gave them suggestions and ideas, they had to take ownership of them and be encouraged to do things in their own way. Telling them what to do would only have resulted in them becoming functionaries, waiting for the next instruction, and taken away any chance of them being more enterprising, thinking for themselves. There was no set format because they were obviously different in their rates of progress. Using the same stimulus on a slow developer as that on a fast tracker would only result in dismay and put us three steps back. If I were an educationalist or, better still, a schoolteacher I would probably know what to do. Again, I had to rely on the theory of 'Do something and if it doesn't work, fix it and then try something else'... Fortunately, I did not have the egoism or arrogance to think that I would always be right. In fact, I wanted to be proved wrong at times, because that would be the breakthrough we were looking for, the point at which I – and they – would know (or, at least, believe) that they were better and wiser than me.

22

THE THOUGHTS OF ST PETER

Obvious things they should know

One of the sheer privileges of writing your own book is that, somewhere towards the end, when you have got all the ideas out of the way that you told the Publisher were ground-breaking and leading edge and all that stuff, and you have basically fulfilled the contract with the reader implicit in the title; and, in any case, you have run out of anecdotes with which to spice up the narrative, while no further consultant-type diagrams come to mind to pad out your revolutionary management theory and business manifesto, you can at last get on to the more important subject of you, your philosophy and the benefits of your lengthy cogitations, expressed as succinct aphorisms, bulleted with all the clarity and concision of 20 years of hindsight.

You can even write paragraphs consisting of one long, compound sentence, if you like. You will be forgiven, by both Publisher and – hopefully – you the reader because, dear reader, what is this writing and reading business all about, if not the getting of wisdom?

So, here are the thoughts of St Peter, expressed in no obvious order, regarding the day-to-day management of a small metalworking business employing seventy people – some of them charge hands whom one wishes would take more responsibility and show more initiative than they have been brought up to do. Some of is a bit technical, a bit metallist. But, even if you just bung the chips in the box at MacDonalds, or answer the phones in a call centre, while the context is wrong, the principles are good, or so I am led to believe,and when it is your turn to grow your own Bubble, you can apply them.

- When taking on a new employee, if you want him to do plenty of overtime, choose the man with a mortgage. Apart from the interview, make sure you check with someone who knows his capabilities whether or not he is any good.

- When selecting a machine tool, choose one with a pedigree and find what it is like in practice from other users. This will tell you more than any salesman would. It would also, probably, have a good resale value in case production and profit from it is not fulfilled.

- Don't be the fool who is busy with work which does not pay.

- With people of the same skills put the one who does the most overtime on the machine with the higher rate. Utilise downtime. Deburr and inspect during production and in large production runs or contract work do a second operation during the cycle time.

- On a production run, look at and evaluate whether specialised tooling can be bought and paid for against that job.

- When estimating a difficult job, estimate on the worst condition because if you quote on the best condition by the Peter Principle the worst will happen. If it doesn't, then you have won a watch.

- Similarly, when giving a delivery to a customer discipline yourself not to promise the best delivery because if it doesn't happen the customer will be disappointed. Whereas, if you make a longer delivery promise and you do it quicker the customer will be pleased and it will still be the same delivery.

- If you are in the wrong and you know it and the irate customer tells you so, do not argue with him but instead agree with him and tell him he is correct in being angry as you would also be in his position. It can sometimes take the wind out of the angry person's sails and may even have your customer apologising for being so angry.

- If you want someone to become involved in a project do not force it on him but win their co-operation and commitment and they will take greater ownership in making the thing work.

- The best form of praise is by stealth. If you can let someone surreptitiously know you thought highly of him through a third party then he knows it is true and not just flattery, empty words or sycophantic.

- Be as honest as you possibly can. You don't need a good memory for your inaccurate statements and you can eliminate games playing. Any game you are playing will be based on morality and done for the best. If you are always truthful it almost follows that you must be more consistent.

- If you do something good or clever, tell people about it. It will make others feel better because good news is better than bad and it should do your reputation no harm, it creates enthusiasm; and others might learn from it.

- Don't blame others for your own mistakes. You will be more thought of if you admit that you're an idiot.

- Do not leave serendipity to chance. Make sure you have a back door or a win-win situation.

- Do not kick people when they are down, it demeans you. Besides, you never know when you might meet them on the way up.

- If you delegate, you have not absolved your responsibility. You are still responsible for that person doing the correct thing. Test him until you can trust him.

- Do not create problems – solve them. If you do have a problem, do not keep it a secret. If no one knows what it is, there is less chance of it being solved.

- If more than one customer is demanding their job from you when you can only satisfy one, give preference to your better customer. It is nonsense to supply a fly-by-night in preference to a good customer even though you have promised him. Unpromise him.

- If you're unhappy with the product you have produced, you should not expect your customer to be happy with it.

- Criticism is best given when things are going well. People can take it better.

- Don't avoid the future by hanging on to the past.

- Have favourites but don't show favouritism.

- Don't catch red herrings but find the facts and source of these and obtain a better chance and clearer picture of knowing what the real problem is.

- Don't assume anything. Assumption is only an excuse for not being on top of your job. As the Yanks say, 'assume makes an ass of u and me'. Yuk!

- If you don't have any problems then you have a problem.

- If you start someone and he is not going to make the grade, get rid of him otherwise you will be shackled with regret.

- When you do not understand something, say so. You may not want to appear a dunderheid but you have a better chance of being one.

- If you want to know how someone would feel in a particular situation then ask yourself how you would feel in that situation.

- When people say they can do anything it normally means they can't do anything.

- Your best customer is the one you make the most money from.

- If you keep losing money from a customer and you can't do anything about it, get rid of them.

Making Good

Jim Good could do anything. He built his own extension. He bred dogs. He played the guitar – Spanish style. He worked with handicapped children. He also had a fair amount of knowledge because he read a lot rather than watch the T.V. in his spare time. His politics, unlike most of us on the shopfloor, tended to be more philosophical than extreme or opinionated. In any circumstance he was minded to do the correct thing, even if he lost out by it. Unlike others in management too set in their ways and a slave to themselves, he was keen to learn and absorbed any and every management book I gave him. Not only was he reading these books, but he would constantly argue against any loose management theory, not in a negative way but in a 'how-would-it-work?' kind-of way. As well as becoming expert on the study of T.Q.M., he would also question me on such diverse things as discounted cash flow in investment appraisal.

When he was promoted and taken off his C.N.C. mill, things immediately began to improve. Having until recently been tied to a machine, his sapiential knowledge allowed him to have a full understanding of the difficulties and problems the operators have. He concentrated on this by streamlining production; by preparing tools and set-ups, and checking computer programs, working methods and planning, making the job easier for the operators and more efficient for the company.

Now, he organises the flow of work to satisfy delivery dates; upholds quality standards; co-ordinates shift work; motivates his men and constantly looks for improvements.

It is not uncommon to see him huddled over a computer screen with our accountant, learning about costs and profits as well as examining how the times and rates of jobs are doing. This commercial awareness will give him a clearer picture of what it's all about and give him more knowledge and facts to enable him to make wiser decisions. It will underline his realism: you must make money, for that's what the game and the fun of the business are all about. Not the money itself, but the making of it.

With this new focus, it will be interesting to see if Jim can fulfil his potential and thereby validate and glorify the Bubble theory.

Although his ability and keenness are beyond doubt, his main stumbling block is likely to be the detractors, the snipers and gossip mongers who will try and drag him back onto a muddy playing field. I am not sure if this is a particularly Scottish trait: we are all 'Jock Tamson's bairns', the Chosen People – and we are damn well going to stay that way. The best way to answer that is to ask ourselves, 'Do we or don't we like to see people getting on?' Jim, so far, applies the best answer to this sniping. He ignores it.

Jim is going through the process of change. To help him he is encouraged to visit other companies and managers to see a broader picture of how things are done elsewhere and to learn from others experiences. He is also encouraged to communicate with customers giving them a personal service and solving their problems.

His is now the most influential voice in how the C.N.C. milling should be run and what direction and strategy will be required for the future. He has a great group of C.N.C. machining centre operators and the latest capital equipment to match. Because of these assets and because he is so good, more demands are made of him to fulfil our expectations. He is encouraged, if he so desires, to give his section it's own identity and if necessary to market it and grow it independently, to make it his own and expand the customer base. Fortunately, this does not go above his head and does not phase him.

Baillie revisited

Most of us were brought into this world by the stork. Baillie Fraser was brought in by a pterodactyl. It would be easy to write him off as having the stereotypical mind that has not been educated and, therefore, has not learned how to think. Admittedly, he has the telltale signs. He glorifies experience and is quick to remind you that, 'It's always been done this way', which robs your chance to think that it could possibly be done a better way. He uses the weight of historical know-how against you. To explore any new ideas renders you a 'poof', or a 'f***ing loony'. He will not argue further than the past and traps you in it. If his knowledge and experience could be transposed to forward mode, he would be miles ahead of his time. Rather than write him off, he became a challenge.

The parable of the hidden talents is the best scenario to examine his contribution and development. Twenty-five years ago we bought a Charmiles spark eroding machine – then, the latest technology from a prestigious Swiss company. Allied to this was the fact that there were few such machines in Scotland, which gave us great market opportunities and potential. It was a machine which cut metal without touching it by electrical discharges between a positive work piece and a negative electrode, the shape of which you created on the work piece. Baillie was working another Swiss machine at the time, an S.I.P. jig borer, and this was the premier skilled job and best machine in subcontract precision engineering at that time. The jig boring operators liked to think they were the Prima Donnas of the machining world and they probably were.

It was therefore fitting that Baillie should be the automatic choice to be trained on the new technology. As was expected, Baillie mastered the skill by doing any job faster than the optimum times recommended by the manufacturers. He made sure he was the quickest and the best – and thus establishing his exclusivity, he staked his claim.

About four years later, one of our apprentices, Colin, ended up in the jig boring department under the auspices of Baillie, as we had no formalised apprentice training at that time. Apprentices just drifted into things through expediency. Baillie's 'boy' was conscientious and hardworking but he was a square peg in a round hole. We probably would have done him a favour by ending his apprenticeship and allowing him the opportunity to pursue another career, and hopefully have greater success. We had done this with a lad who had nine O levels but was completely handless. He went on to become a quantity surveyor. We didn't, and Baillie, to his credit, took care of this, the weakest member of our brood. For many years he nurtured and cajoled and bullied him into becoming a first class jig borer.

Now the master of both the new technology and the highly skilled jig boring, this was the foundations of his empire. Twenty-five years later, Baillie is still working the same spark eroder and Colin the same jig borer.

As Time flashed by for the rest of us, we did try to make more profitable use of the spark eroder by doing plastic injection moulding tools, which had growth potential. But Baillie made sure we were totally dependent on him and he would not teach anyone else to use his machine. In fact it became a myth in the company that Baillie's spark eroder would only start if you used his cabinet as a big drum and sang the 'Sash' to it, badly. Undoubtedly, management were partly to blame for Baillie's lack of progress, letting him go on dwelling in his cave rather than trying to coax him out. But management are doing something now by moving Colin on, because he is under-utilised. Baillie insists that he is not ready yet and still has 'a bit to learn'. Baillie's 'boy' is now 38 years old...

Colin no longer shares a cave with Baillie; and, to all us normal intelligent beings, it seems we should mentally castigate Baillie for keeping him in there with him so long. That is until we find out that Baillie may have been perfectly justified and correct in this approach, It turned out that Colin, like many highly intelligent people, was a bit of a scatterbrain. Baillie kept him focused. This was justifiable because during this time Colin did not show any evidence or desire to progress. In a tight-knit working environment, there was no opportunity for Colin no matter how much he may have wanted to progress.

Rather than embrace the opportunities we were trying to give him, Baillie's life revolved around the perpetuation of Baillie the character. Revelling in his dinosaur appellation, he is hardly going to change now and all the work over the last two years in trying to convince him to move forward has been to no avail. He will not progress. He will not come out of his cave. Macho man has won.

Baillie is, however, nurturing the life blood of our company by ruggedly developing our young talent and skills for our future. He is now determined to make his boys as good and better than he was. And this emphasises my earlier point about money and loyalty. You don't just dump a man like Baillie as an insult to late 20th century management theory. Lost cause he may be, cantankerous and pig-headed perhaps —but he is a hugely valuable member of the team, in the hardest possible sense. Every company should have one.

23

LOST BOTTLES

The bubble blowers are still showing few signs of ambition, but there is plenty of evidence of how hard they are working, without demanding or claiming too much reward. 'Just bring in the work and we will do it'... Hang on, isn't this where I came in? Have they learned nothing? Where's the *vision*? Where are the star players who should be emerging by now —the Whiz-kid? The Entrepreneur? The Organiser? The Accountant?

More to the point, where is my *Successor?*

They have all drifted away from doing weekly sheets, 'personal development plans', Investors in People and all the other managerial fads and fashions that masquerade as drivers for change. If you are focused on the main task and are constantly improving your process, the new management techniques are peripheral. They all share their same aim in any case, the quest for continuous improvement, dressed up in a variety of fancy outfits. So the fact that our people were no longer interested did not disappoint me. Maybe they had found their own Mantra for success? In a pig's eye.

Within a smaller company, there is less need for formalised documentation. The measures needed to see how well you are doing can be made blatantly obvious. The lines of communication are shorter. The temptation is always just to 'get on with the job', rather than muck about with standard procedures. Consequently, a lot of consultancy theory, British Standard-certified management practice and book learning goes by the board; it's just not 'how we do it'. If you are making profits, why bother analysing everything?

For this reason, perhaps, some rare occasions have unfortunately occurred when the charge hands have reverted to type.

One particular instance was after a holiday period, when the work intake dried up. After the usual barrack-room gossip and murmuring on the shop floor about 'no salesmen', 'management not doing enough work' and 'too many non-production workers', it was Baillie in fact who called a meeting of the charge hands and myself to find out what our future was and what guarantees I could give them. Now they were being pressurised by the work force, they had to act like managers and leaders and hold the line against this kind of irrational panic. The flow of work is, and never has been, constant in subcontract or in many other areas of manufacturing, come to that. They knew the situation. They knew I wasn't concerned, and that it was only a blip — but they still insisted collectively, in spite of my openness and lines of communication, on receiving my personal reassurance that everything was under control. In short, they lost their bottle.

In my anger, brought on by disappointment, I set up the meeting room with all the chairs in line against the back wall instead of around the table, as we usually did; thinking that, if they were going to act like wee boys, then I would treat them like wee boys. Ignoring this obvious insult, they threw me the same worries the shopfloor had, wanting management guarantees that everything would be okay. In reply, I scorned their need for a meeting and their lack of resolve and fortitude. I then sympathised with their fears, which they thought were totally valid, by offering them all a cuddle. I think they got the message, although I was rejected with a sore punch in the ribs from Baillie when I tried to put my arms around him.

Where are the stars?

In spite of my having created all the right conditions for the bubble blowers to thrive, and in spite of the general increase in satisfaction, rise in profits and so on, and in spite of some cracking individual performances, no genuine star players have yet appeared. Perhaps I am just frustrated by the amount of time it has taken. Perhaps there have not been sufficient business opportunities to allow things to happen quicker. Nevertheless, no entrepreneurs have emerged. What we do have are competent managers, who are more able and more professionally able to take on larger projects to service our larger customers and give us strength in depth. They can be trusted to do the job, to deal with the customers, to price the jobs profitably and to control the work flow. Maybe this is as far as it goes? Do I really have a right to expect any more? I don't know, we are out of the park here and still very much feeling our way.

Of course, if you believe in fairy tales or are a practitioner of positive thinking, you already know that all the charge hands live happily ever after and go on to run large multinational corporations or become billionaire arbitrageurs, donating half their fortunes to the development of the Third World... Even if you don't, you may want them to succeed and excel as you are not close enough to the shop floor to be jealous or malevolent, Unfortunately, most of us have to deal with reality.

One step forward

The reality is that stardom never knocks for most people. These men have had no formal higher education; no managerial training or experience. They were not born whiz-kids or entrepreneurs. In fact, they were at a considerable environmental disadvantage, being set in their ways virtually from birth, if not before. (In fact, I should not be surprised if some scientist does not soon discover a gene which codes for this programming. Otherwise, what is the evolutionary imperative? 'Quick, lads. Let's stay rooted to the spot and maybe that sabre-toothed tiger won't notice us'? A likely story.) It would in fact be preposterous for us to expect them to have a propensity for creative genius. All they have done is taken one step forward, with the occasional two-step lurch the other way... I should get off their backs. Who are we to cast the first stone?

24

REACTIONS

From the outset, top management were envious, secretive, insecure and, at best, ambivalent towards this whole process of job enrichment for the lower orders. They hung on grimly, hoping to see the thing fall apart, rewarding themselves with the chance to say they knew it would never work. Just to make sure, they missed no opportunity to undermine and rubbish the process in private.

It was frankly annoying to find, for instance, that even their closest customers had no idea of what we were attempting to do. We were working in total isolation from the rest of Scottish industry, apparently. Even when we gained national news coverage for the experiment, they did not ask their business acquaintances if they had seen the newspaper article about the company or understood what we were trying to achieve. Even their active criticism and discussion of the program could have made a welcome contribution. Alas, they contributed nothing.It was a virtual precondition of success that everyone in the company should share the same vision. Instead, I had to soldier on in this fog of apathy which they generated. Although it was evident that I was unwavering in my determination to change the culture, they only began to have any credence in our home-grown Bubble theory when it started to filter back to them from other sources outside the company. Familiarity does indeed breed contempt.

In fact, the shopfloor man more readily accepted the vision; and, unlike management, wanted to know things. How were the charge hands to be motivated; or, in other words, were there to be monetary rewards? Were they qualified to participate? And if so, how were they to be chosen? How would they be assessed? The more awkward or difficult the question, the more pleased I was. Motivated as they may have been by a tinge of fear and envy, nevertheless these men at least were prepared to debate the issue and help to bring up any problems, so giving us a chance of solving them. They fully understood the Bubble theory and in general saw it as a means to growth, wherein they would have more opportunities if others developed and grew the company with them. They accepted it as a valid means of looking to the future, even if it meant abandoning past certainties and the apathetic reliance on 'management' for all their rewards.

A growing belief

Outside support was also a great contributing factor in gaining acceptance for the Bubble theory. The more people from whatever walk of life who showed enthusiasm and encouragement, the more management began to accept, if not exactly to believe in, what we were trying to do. A doctor at the local golf course approached one of our charge hands and wanted to know about the Bubble theory. Management consultants (or, at least, their clients) paid good money for the privilege of bringing managers and executives from leading edge companies to question us. The management of our largest oil customer came down from Aberdeen, solely to find out what we were doing. Others expressed sentiments that they wished their own companies were as open and forward thinking and practised what they preached... After the newspaper article, someone taunted one of our senior managers by shouting across the street to ask him why he did not have a bubble around him?

It all helped to gain acceptability for the theory and practice of bubble blowing throughout the company, if not yet exactly finding the fabled G-spot with senior management.

25

CONCLUSION

Jim Good, our great white hope, is flying. Not only is he running his bubble with great efficiency and initiative bur he is innovative and entrepreneurial. He has his team buzzing. He has kept them involved and got them to contribute to running and developing the section and themselves. Embracing authority and responsibility he has fashioned a 'dream team'. All managerial decisions are his. He has developed customers and gives them such good service that they queue to give him more work. He has selected and invested in machinery wisely and profitably, anticipating every shifting demand of our market. His bubble is growing at 25 per cent per annum and needs more space, which he wants to go beyond our existing premises because we are holding him back.

There is, unfortunately, one sad thing about this Jim – he does not exist. I wish he did. But I have to confess: he is purely fictitious, a composite of all that is best and most to be desired in the shopfloor men; not all of whom were willing to be portrayed, warts and all, in this affectionate tribute to their undoubted skills and eccentricities.

Jim

Jim Durnion, our passive aggressor, on the other hand has an agnostic outlook. He appreciates the opportunities of Bubble theory in an ideal world but does not see any opportunities for himself, except in the traditional way of gaining promotion in the old hierarchical organisation. Although exposed to customers with the opportunity to develop business, he is by necessity too preoccupied with manufacturing and doing a good technical job, which is his forte. He is, however, good with customers. More exposure to growing markets and the rewards of bring in business will eventually overcome his agnosticism, and he will be converted, although he still will not believe it.

Davie

The highly-strung Davie Semple is still avidly absorbing all the latest fads in computers and new technology and has now immersed himself in the electronics market, which we are breaking into. His mercurial traits do not lend themselves to higher management and leadership but are precious in his role as the Boffin. From a C.N.C. vertical milling machine operator to Boffin in two years is no mean feat and must be considered a great success.

David

David McLaughlin, our tame 'bastard', has made great strides but is stuck on the plane he has reached . He is the biggest disciple of the Bubble theory, believing implicitly in its role in improving the company and giving opportunity to many from the shopfloor. The trouble is, he is too comfortable in his success. His ambition is blunted by using time as his ally, waiting for people to retire, for his time to come, rather than driving for himself and becoming that self-interested 'bastard' we all know and love. Like a parrot needing to be pushed off his perch, he has unfulfilled potential. He must do more for himself and the company.

Stewart

The 'Prince of Darkness', Stewart Miller, is also a believer. His comments are usually critical of those not taking opportunities or not appreciating them. He is well aware of how and what others should be doing in their development. He can easily do this from the vantage point of his Services role; wherein, to his mind (and mine), his own progress is limited by not being in the pressure cooker of Production. This will have to be changed, because he too is capable of much more. After two years of bubble blowing, he is undoubtedly happier and more developed.

Peter

Peter Tait, our Union man and philosopher, is both the least progressed and the most progressed. The least, because he is still working full-time on his milling machine, looking after the smallest bubble — one which shows no signs of growth. He needs no defence, because no opportunities have arisen and I have not conjured any up for him. He is the most progressed mentally, however. In looking for opportunities, he realised we needed a new brochure, which he set about producing. With great initiative he produced a much-acclaimed communication, minimalist in its design, with some great copy lines, such as:

> *Excellence is an attitude. Excellence is in the approach to the task. Excellence is having the vision to make the very best possible use of all available resources.*

He also incorporates the subliminal message of, 'The difference is the attitude'. After thirty years in manufacture he is totally complimentary to the Bubble theory in breaking the mould and giving opportunity, although he himself has not visibly taken off. At fifty-five years of age his mind remains active, and it's vital that I find him something to satisfy his ability, no matter what his age.

Baillie

Baillie Fraser, our unreconstructed dinosaur, has not changed. Baillie Fraser will never change. Baillie Fraser has lived, will live forever in the Jurassic Park of the human mind.

Raymond

Raymond Davies is our biggest success. Something he always had the potential for, but never the opportunity. Now, he is about to fulfil all the promise that the Bubble theory holds out. He has taken on the heavyweight task of diversifying the business, out of pure precision machining and its markets, and into the quality electronics market.

Assiduously, stealthily and quietly working away on his own (what did I say about team players?), he is on the verge of making the breakthrough which will put the company on a higher plane and create exponential growth. Raymond, as I have said,was always capable but a way had to be found to give him the opportunity and freedom to fulfil that latent talent. There is not much more to say about Raymond, as I think he would succeed in whatever he did and therefore he doesn't prove our Bubble theory, other than to note that it gave him the opportunity, whereas other cultures in other companies might never have done so.

Moving on

Without exception (apart from Baillie), all the charge hands agree that the experiment and effort have been good for the company and that it is a different and better company than it was two years ago. From their own subjective viewpoint they have to admit, without reservation, to having moved on and are better and happier for the effort and transition. We have tried to take the blinkers off the shopfloor man. Whether or not we shall succeed, it is the experiment itself that is important. When dealing with abstracts like 'culture' and 'change', there are really no absolutes. You can stick your own flags in the minefield; but the mines are smart, they are constantly shifting position. And there is no limit to the size of the field.

Bubble theory therefore is just that: theory. And theories are there to be applied – or shot down in flames. Your own situation and the way you apply the theory will be very different; and no doubt, when you come to write your own book two years from now, you will (hopefully) have a very different story to tell. The only sage advice I can give you, in my new-found role as management consultant is this:

Remain true to your vision.

Not yet, perhaps...

THE END

POSTSCRIPT

Alone in the lighthouse

It is now two years since I originally drafted the manuscript of this book; and, before I give my opinion on the state of play and how things have progressed (quite gratifyingly, as it happens) I've got another story to tell you.

The Technical Director of a multinational visited us recently (as they are wont to do). It was his first visit in two years, and he was amazed. Not, he explained, with the undoubted improvements on the shop floor, but with the calibre of the personnel. He had a confession to make, he said. He had previously not rated our management. But now, he admitted, professionally at least, they were his equals! This view, freely expressed, spoke volumes for the progress we had made. These men he was complimenting in a rather bemused fashion were not just the 'jumped-up chargehands' (his expression, not mine!), they included top management; those whose hearts and minds had been so difficult to influence, in our drive for cultural change.

From the day I began the process, it had seemed that the floor had dropped away beneath my feet. There was no solid ground; no guidelines to follow,no certainty that what I was doing was even right.I had been in a kind of foggy, grey 'limbo' land. If I had taken the advice of 'H.G.V.', Lawrie Spence, our Consultant, doubtless there would have been cuts and 'blood on the floor'. Rather than a knife, however, I had preferred to use a walking stick, at least until I could find my feet. I had given my charge hands walking sticks, too.

Now, it seemed, they had thrown them away – and it hadn't even needed a trip to Lourdes.

I had trusted them to find and do the right things, and they had not let me down. They had stuck to, and developed, their strengths; for, it was their strengths we wanted, not their weaknesses. Now, they are using those strengths in a focused way, by concentrating on the development and growth of the company, rather than on their own, narrow agendas. They take responsibility for growing their bubbles, and get on with things, rather than have me do them. They solve problems, rather than create them; or worse, delegate them to me! They also guide, help and motivate others In fact, they have left me with remarkably little to do. I have no monkeys on my back. And, if the truth be told, it's a bit lonely here in the lighthouse.

The fruits of Change

I suppose that, if you are not part of this company, its processes and markets; if, in short, you have strayed unwittingly into the pages of this book out of sheer curiosity, and have hung on this long, the big question you will want to ask me now is: 'Yes, but what effect has this quantum shift in the cultural patterns of your business (or some such flowery phrase) actually had on your <u>bottom line</u>?

In a manufacturing environment that has continued to decline, with the loss of major customers to the subcontracting industry, companies like British Steel, Caterpillar, Cummins Engines and Anderson Long having all departed, Main Tool during the same period has posted average growth of 25 per cent *per annum* over the past three years.

Yet we still don't have even one salesman; while, to the chagrin no doubt of our highly-targeted Bank Manager, we have done it all without 'gearing'... at least, of the financial sort.

As for the others:

About one year ago, Raymond wanted to invest in a new machine tool costing £50,000. He asked me to do an investment appraisal, which I happily did; but unhappily,it showed that the machine was not worth buying. Raymond challenged me: where were all my theories now, since he wanted and needed that machine because he *knew* it was the way forward, and I was the one who wouldn't progress? I immediately gave way, conceding that his gut feel took precedence over my figures. It soon became apparent that he was right, and my figures weren't... Mathematical analysis seldom takes account of all the conditions that obtain in the real world, whereas we are born with instincts that include not only the ability to do calculations,but also to incorporate a whole range of extra-sensory data; adding quality, as well as quantity, to the equation we call life.

Another time, though, Raymond wavered. He complained to me about my 'leadership' qualities, saying I wasn't giving enough 'direction'. It just so happened that I had been reading one of Heller's management books, in which he has a few inspirational pages on how, unless a leader lets others lead, he will always have followers... I showed this to Raymond. Two months later, he opened up a new toolmaking division in leased premises across the road, taking with him Davie Semple, the Technical and Design Manager, and Jim Durnion, the Production Manager.

It was a total vindication of all that I had stood and fought for. I wasn't having anyone or anything get in his way; but I asked only one thing of him. If you, the reader, wish to jump to the obvious conclusion, and tell me that that was 'profits', well, I am sorry to disappoint you; but I am not about to abandon my newly-held convictions now. To save you reading the book all over again, I will tell you that what I asked of Raymond was this: to *be successful...* Making a profit is only a discounted facet of something I wanted of him that is far greater. Profits are only one incidental measure of success: I wanted to see Raymond's new bubble rise ever-higher into the sky, and many others along with it.

As for the others, well, a bit of recession has put them on hold; but the legacy of 'Jim Good' is evident in them, and they will grow and prosper, both for the company and themselves. My only anxiety is that we shall need a new 'principle' for our 'Socialist', Peter Tait: since how can such capable people succeed and prosper and yet continue to refuse to wear their wealth and ambition on their sleeve?

Baillie Fraser remains, of course, like an increasingly precious antique. It is worth a fortune, but you can't do anything with it! Yet you would never part with it because you cherish it so. Baillie is a large part of the culture and soul of the company, a man surely destined to become a legend.

Overall, therefore, the table has been turned. Shopfloor Man is now confident, focused and self-directed; while I am the one who is 'out of his comfort zone', for I have nothing better to do now than write books. The less I do, it seems, the more money I make; which is how the men want it, of course...

You may write my epitaph now. To quote a former Tory chancellor, Gordon Lamont, on leaving office under something of a media cloud: *'Je ne regrette rien'*...